THE B

"*The Business Artist* captures the essence of our times, where human creativity intersects with digital transformation. It is a great read for anyone looking to harness the growth-stimulating power of innovation."

– BILL MCDERMOTT, CEO at ServiceNow & former CEO of SAP

"Adam is the rare breed of bird that we need today—one who understands how to embrace all that technology and business can bring to the world without losing your soul. This book will give you the road map for navigating the world before us."

– PETER MULFORD, Global Partner & Chief Innovation Officer at BTS

"Never before has a book so perfectly captured the importance of creativity in delivering business results and leading a fully human life. For salespeople, this is your guide to inspire innovation with customers. For leaders, you've heard about 'authentic leadership' as a buzzword, but Boggs brings you the playbook."

– ANDREW DORNON, Co-Founder, Forge Strategy Partners

"*The Business Artist* is filled with practical wisdom. Boggs shares innovative strategies from his experience, showing how to ignite team creativity and harness collective intelligence. This book is a must-read for those who seek to transform ideas into impactful business solutions."

– MATT PROSTKO, VP of Product, TaskHuman

"Through *The Business Artist*, Boggs masterfully demonstrates the art of using metaphors and storytelling in business. His engaging examples show how these techniques can create lasting impressions and effectively communicate the core message of a product or idea."

– CATHY HITE, Former Global Head of Sales Enablement, SAP

"This book is a compelling exploration of the convergence of art and business, championing creativity and human connection as the keys to transforming corporate landscapes. Adam Boggs illustrates how adopting an improvisational, jazz-like approach in business can lead to innovative leadership and authentic engagement. It's a must-read for anyone seeking to infuse artistic creativity into their professional life."

— **DOUGLAS FERGUSON**, President at Voltage Control, Entrepreneur and Human-Centered Technologist

"The Business Artist illustrates the importance of blending creativity and business with an innovative framework on how the artist in everyone can bring value to the business world through practical application. After all, we are all artists!"

— **TRAVIS JONES**, Former Global Head of Enablement, Autodesk

"Dispelling the common belief that art and business are entirely separate domains, *The Business Artist* intelligently proves otherwise. By exploring the coexistence of creative thinking and business outcomes, individuals can experience significant personal and professional growth. Those who dare to step out of their comfort zones and embrace this approach will witness a remarkable progression in their lives."

— **BART FANELLI**, Former CRO of Outreach and Head of Sales Enablement at Splunk, Founder of Skillibrium

"As someone who has made a career of challenging the status quo, demanding industry evolution, and pushing for the inclusion of diverse views and perspectives, I appreciate how *The Business Artist* encourages people to forge new paths in business. The book extends readers an invitation to embrace innovation, reject imitation, and create a lasting impact in their industry."

— **SARAH SPAIN**, espnW Writer, ESPN Radio Host & TV Personality

"Whether you're just starting or a seasoned pro, *The Business Artist* offers invaluable insights for sales professionals. Filled with tips on creativity, storytelling, and unique sales acumen, it will reshape how you connect with clients and close deals."

– **WILL NICOL**, VP of Sales and Pre-Sales, Autodesk and BricsysCAD

"In the wake of generative AI, *The Business Artist* emerges as a critical guide, underscoring the increasing importance of business artistry. As technology reshapes our landscape, this book illuminates how our unique human creativity and problem-solving skills become not only valuable but also essential in harnessing the power of AI."

– **AKIO AIDA**, Enterprise Sales, Grammarly

"As an artist myself, I often get questions about how I made the transition from performer to business professional. In *The Business Artist*, my long-time friend and colleague, Adam Boggs, explains how the two are so beautifully in sync as a guide to success. Taking a human-centered approach to business decisions, integrating storytelling and emotional connection to leadership, and debunking the myth that best practices are better than creativity and innovation—that's what makes this book something I would encourage you to pick up."

– **JENNIFER TURNER**, Director, HR Strategy Consultant
to Alphabet Companies at Google

THE BUSINESS ARTIST

A Human Approach to Sales, Storytelling, and Creativity in a Data-Driven World

ADAM BOGGS

WITH KENT SANDERS

SPECIAL INVITATION

I'd like to personally invite you to download *The Business Artist Action Guide*. This free resource will help you put what you've learned in *The Business Artist* into practice. You can access it via the link below.

HTTPS://ADAMBOGGS.IO/BONUS

DEDICATION

To my Latin Sensation, my wife and boogaloo,
Chrissi Hernandez:

In our sixteen plus years together, your artistic spirit has
opened my eyes to beauty I once overlooked. I remember
the fading sunset you first showed me, describing the
theory of morphing orange to purple as we drove home one
Christmas night from Nana and Grandjack's house.

On our global adventures, your wisdom illuminated each
museum we explored, unveiling artistic styles and influences
invisible to my untrained eye. My mind sprinted to absorb
it all— always curious.

You nurtured my desire to uncover today's emerging
aesthetics, and to grasp how we might apply this awareness
to business and life. Without you, this book would not exist.

You have made the world a richer canvas by being open-
minded, slow to judge, and quick to appreciate. Your free
spirit tempers my intensity with calm. As my compass and
my best friend, you push me to grow yet keep me grounded.

With infinite love and gratitude, this book is for you. Here's
to a lifetime more of sunsets and adventures together.

TABLE OF CONTENTS

INTRODUCTION

What is art? It's a question that has intrigued humanity for thousands of years. From primitive cave paintings in France to digital artwork created by artificial intelligence (AI), we continue to ask what role creative expression plays in our past, present, and future.

To me, art is the process where you freely express yourself through some kind of medium. That medium could be a physical object like a sculpture or a painting. It could be a service you perform, such as mowing lawns or cutting hair. Or it can be expressed through creative forms you can't touch, but can enjoy with your ears and eyes, such as music or film. Whatever the medium, the main idea of art is to share yourself in a form that other people can enjoy and experience.

But how does that happen in the corporate world, where creative thinking usually takes a backseat to more pressing concerns like sales quotas and quarterly earnings reports? How can artists make a unique contribution to the world of business? How can we use storytelling to better connect with our clients, customers, and colleagues? And what role will artists continue to play in a world where algorithms, big data, and AI seem to dominate every discussion?

These questions and more are what *The Business Artist* is all about.

Creativity has played a critical role in driving human culture forward. We have crossed oceans, built skyscrapers, harnessed religion, and taken the first of many steps to explore our solar system and beyond. We accomplished all this through creative thinking. It's time for us to remember once again how special that creative impulse is and why it sets us apart as human beings.

This creative power is available to you as well, no matter what your job or business. I'll share stories of other business leaders and salespeople who have harnessed this creative impulse so you have a clear pathway forward. And I'll give you an opportunity to explore tools and techniques to get into *flow*—that all-important artistic term you'll learn more about.

We're also going to talk about what it means to be a Business Artist moving forward. This is not just a one-time process. I hope this book will be a toolkit that you can come back to often—a catalyst that ignites your desire to share your own stories and move forward in community with other Business Artists.

It's easier to judge than to accept critique. It's easier to consume than create. Why? Because companies have created technology that allows people to follow repeatable, scalable processes for what to sell and how to answer questions. I want to show you how to break out of this pattern yet still make use of the best of these processes as a Business Artist.

Business is Like Jazz

In my research with technology and business leaders, I've found that the most successful people inside companies, the leaders who are driving the highest performance among people, are not necessarily the ones imitating others. You might even say they are stubborn.

Why? Because they challenged the status quo. They create in cycles. They have creative minds. They're inspiring to work for. They know themselves, and they know how to flex their own innate human strengths.

These are the kinds of leaders who are on a call with a customer, and when they are finished, one of their team members looks at them in awe and says, "How did you do that? How did you connect with that customer? Why did you share that story or know where to take that conversation?"

Then, they will shrug their shoulders and say, "I don't know. I was improvising. I was in a state of flow. I wasn't playing a memorized track or reading a script."

To put it in musical terms, what they're really saying is this: *I wasn't reading from the sheet music. I was going with the flow. I was playing jazz.*

That's what we're going to talk about in this book—the importance of being an artist in the business environment you support. I want to effectively show you how to use stories and illustrate how beneficial they can be for you and your life. But we're also going to talk about why we've reached a tipping point that makes being a Business Artist more important than ever.

Technology has brought us to a place where we are no longer acting as human beings. We've lost our sense of empathy. We've lost our fulfillment from creating. We've lost our ability to step outside of our own opinions and objectively look at other people's creative work.

Instead, we just judge. We have become a world of critics. All you have to do to see for yourself is to look at any social media platform. No matter which ones you use, you always have the ability to show your approval by "liking" something, responding with an icon that shows your emotion, or making a comment. Today it seems we spend much more energy judging than actually creating.

Throughout this book, you'll see music or jazz metaphors pop up. That's not just because I love the analogy when applies to business. It's also because music is part of who I am. I got into music when I was young and started understanding that I could play music just like everybody else by reading sheet music. But it didn't really work for me. I memorized how to play songs, and all of a sudden, I could play on hotel pianos and impress people. But music didn't click for me until I learned the theory behind it.

You don't need to understand music theory or play an instrument to benefit from *The Business Artist*. A creative approach to life and business involves so much more than music. However, as you read the book, I encourage you to put on a little jazz in the background—perhaps some classic artists like Miles Davis and Bill Evans or any number of newer artists—to help set the mood.

My Early Years

Now that I've shared a bit about my goals for the book, you may be wondering, *Who is this Adam Boggs guy?* Let me take a few moments to share some of my story so you'll see where I'm coming from and how it's led to this book.

My father was a salesman. He grew up selling fencing door to door, then inside steel companies, where he rose to senior management ranks. He traveled a lot but always came home with great stories and a copy of the *Wall Street Journal* so we could discuss and debate topics.

We grew up in a middle-class household of four kids, always with one golden retriever or goldendoodle. My best friend has been, and always will be, my identical twin brother, Eric. We played every sport together. I was a catcher, and he was a pitcher in baseball. I was an outside hitter, and he was a setter in volleyball.

Whether it was team sports like baseball or volleyball, individual sports like track or swimming, or even doing schoolwork, we always competed against each other. Since we had the same anatomical gifts of DNA, the only real separation was will and effort, right? Or so we thought.

I always had a love of learning growing up, but I realized there is a limit to the number of times you can ask "Why?" to an adult before they become annoyed. I learned a lot from my mom, who was a teacher and guidance counselor. I'd learn from her and always have heavy debates with Dad. My older brother went on to become a college professor. My little sister became an elementary school teacher. My twin brother and I are consultants, with my focus on teaching adults.

When I was in high school in the late 1990s, I got my first taste of technology and entrepreneurship. My brother and I took Cisco certification training offered in our small high school in northwest Indiana. Then we went on to start a small company with our friends Erik and Jerry, installing broadband internet infrastructure in schools and small businesses. We'd run the cabling, configure the routers and switches, and hook it up to a Tier-2 fiber line. This was all before Wi-Fi existed, of course.

Now I just laugh at the amount of copper wiring we ran that is sitting unused in walls and ceilings. I'll never forget the feeling of creating something at such a young age. It gave us all a sense of purpose and creative autonomy. We became aware of what's possible when you get into a flow state where you are energized, focused, and maximizing your strengths as a team while learning new skills.

In many ways, this book is an extension of the dreams we had as kids and what we were able to accomplish. It was a time before the world became obsessed with growth through systematizing everything and putting structure around every decision, process, and framework.

My brother and I, along with our two friends, went to Purdue and studied computer technology together, although we went in different directions once we landed at a big university. My brother and I doubled up our majors with business degrees, taking nearly all of the same classes and interning in the same places, with me graduating six months before him. (Take that, Eric!) We're still competitive.

Going to school with someone who looked like me had its perks. Since we're both outgoing individuals who love to meet new people, we had a natural icebreaker when a girl or guy came up to one of us and said, "Hey! Great to see you again." Maybe we had never met this person before but decided to improvise and play along, or just tell them straight up, "You must have met my brother," and embarrass them. You can guess which option I took more often.

From Consulting to Meahana

I've always enjoyed the energy that comes from other people. Fortunately, I've been able to put this energy to good use in my work life.

For most of my professional career, I worked in sales and consulting for some of the world's largest and most innovative technology clients, including Google, Salesforce, SAP, Autodesk, Splunk, Cisco, and many others. I've led engagements and workshops on every continent except for Antarctica and have always been fascinated with observing what drives individual and team performance.

The world seems to be driving toward more data, standardization, and optimization. However, I've found that the people who are thriving do so in a work culture that matches their style, gives them a chance to bring artistry into their work, and encourages collaboration with colleagues.

I believe that as AI automates routine work, our human values will shift toward unlocking creative potential through collaboration. The only issue is that the tools to do that well don't exist yet. Everything is another derivative of a virtual whiteboard with some clunky AI features or polls. Sure, you get input and contribution, but this is not the way to capture that *lightning in a bottle* you get from live collaboration.

This is why I left my high-paying consulting role to start Meahana, a new collaboration platform that uses a radically different approach we call "idea flow," which is necessary to activate the full wisdom of teams. There is no whiteboard (crazy, I know!), but instead, you link together a series of activities (micro apps) that are tailored to meet specific goals.

The activities can range from complex and sophisticated, like branching brainstorms, tech evaluations, or scenario simulations, to simple or focused activities such as rankings or polls. The magic is that all of these activities and their input can be linked to each other in any way your creativity desires. For example, you might want to do a sequence of three events, such as an brainstorming to capture ideas, prioritizing items to narrow down the list, or creating an action plan to calendar your next steps for the top-rated idea.

Meahana is the combination of two Hawaiian words: *mea* and *hana*. *Mea* refers to an object, person, or thing. *Hana* means to work or to create. Both this book and my business share a common goal: to unlock creativity by providing individuals with the mental, physical, and technological tools to drive their artistic vision.

The Human Touch

My experience in sales, consulting, and starting Meahana has helped me to see what is missing. Time and again, I've seen employees asked to just fall in line. I've seen accreditations based on certifying people who can sell a product because they memorized a product script. I've interviewed hundreds of customers and salespeople, trying to figure out what drives the most joyful and impactful sales conversations.

Often, it's the human connection—the human conversation—that makes the difference. It's more than the product pitch or slide deck. One customer I talked to said, "Sometimes I think the biggest barrier to the buyer-seller relationship is their language."

Language has to go through a filter. It doesn't always get translated in the way we think. The many conversations I've had with those salespeople and customers have helped me see one thing: The way we are doing business is repeatable and scalable, but lacks the human touch so desperately needed in the world today.

Sellers are constantly burdened with the challenge of figuring out how to talk, how to show up, and what slides to use. It's like me as a young kid sitting down with sheet music, feeling overwhelmed. All I really wanted to do was learn how to play in my own style and connect with an audience.

Now, one of my favorite things to do is to sit down at a hotel piano and just start playing while surrounded by strangers. I like to watch and react to what's working and not working. I don't have to be burdened by playing a memorized song I have in my back pocket.

Today I can translate that same sense of flow and curiosity into my sales conversations. I've been very successful at selling differently in each situation. I use distinctive forms of communication depending on the particular person or audience. Sometimes I use video proposals instead of PowerPoint decks because I know they might translate better to that particular person or audience. I may text message a client or get on social media. I've never followed a specific playbook.

If you're tired of following a script in your sales conversations and business—more importantly, if you're tired of following a script in your life—then you're in the right place.

Maybe you're afraid to try something new. You're not sure how your colleagues, supervisors, customers, or clients might react. You're used to following the same scripts you've always used. Maybe everyone around you is following the script, and it feels intimidating to break away from the norm. Whatever your fears and concerns, I'm here to show you the way and give you actionable steps at every turn.

The Journey Ahead

In *The Business Artist*, we'll use the metaphor of music to map out the journey of where we've been, where we're going, and how we will get there.

In Part 1, we'll explore why business seems so **dissonant** and out of tune today. It's the "why" of the book. Part 1 lays the foundation for why we need a new approach to business and sales. We must understand the nature of the problem before we can talk about solutions. I'll also explore what dissonance means (tension, harmony, or clashing between notes) and why that is a great metaphor for today's business conditions.

In Part 2, we'll look at **melody**, the pathway of the Business Artist. This section will describe why we need Business Artists and how to become one. We will also think about why *melody* (the rhythmic movement of notes in an ordered progression) is an appropriate metaphor for this approach.

Then, in Part 3, we will tie everything together in **harmony** to give you practical strategies and takeaways. This book is all about relationships. Relationships are like jazz, where there is a natural ebb and flow. Life and business are constantly evolving. We must not only get comfortable with change—we need to learn how to navigate it. With that in mind, Part 3 will focus on how to navigate change in five concentric circles where we operate as Business Artists.

The old way of doing business relies on standardized, outdated approaches to selling that focus on confrontation, manipulation, and treating all customers the same way. Instead, we will call for a new approach that centers on relationships, empathy, and collaboration.

This is not a playbook or a cookbook where you follow the recipe, and it will turn out the same way every time. *The Business Artist* will challenge you to think about your own work, to bring in your own ideas, and to wrestle with them. It's not a self-help book, a strengths finder book, or a personality assessment book.

After reading this book, I hope that you experience not only your business life but also your art differently. I want you to look at music, movies, theater, painting, architecture, and more and ask the question, "What was the artist trying to do?" I want you to be able to appreciate the effort and intention of the creator even if you didn't particularly enjoy something.

The end goal of art is not to create art for art's sake. It's to impact the person who sees, hears, and experiences it. We ultimately create for others.

In the same way, I want you to think about how you engage with your clients or customers. How do you want them to experience your conversations, presentations, or slide decks in a way that's emotionally connected to them?

If you listen to jazz, you have probably noticed that it always comes back to a theme or motif. When people first experience jazz, it sounds like chaos. They can't tell what happened to the melody partway through the song. But it almost always comes back to the theme. The musicians may be improvising, riffing, and playing off one another, but it's always within the context of the song.

That's the goal of *The Business Artist*—to help you find the theme, the motif—the pathway forward amidst the chaos today. Thanks for taking the journey with me.

PART 1

DISSONANCE

WHY BUSINESS SEEMS SO OUT OF TUNE TODAY

HOW DID WE GET HERE?

We all see the world through our individual lenses. You only need to be on social media for a few seconds before you encounter different perspectives on an issue. We disagree on nearly everything these days, and we're not afraid to share it.

However, there is one thing we can probably all agree on: Business isn't what it used to be. We live in a different world than the one we grew up in. Everything is changing at a faster pace than ever, including the way we do business and engage with each other. Commerce is in danger of becoming more impersonal and commoditized with every passing year.

We'll get to some suggestions and solutions a little later in the book. But before we do that, it's important to take a step back and look at the bigger picture. In this chapter, I invite you to journey with me as we consider how business became so impersonal in the first place.

Just like you, I've experienced the coldness of data-driven decision-making firsthand. My first dose of reality came at age nineteen as a college student.

A Personal Experience with the Impersonal

I went to Purdue to get a computer engineering degree with a minor in business. One year, I interned at 3M, the large Minnesota company that makes sticky notes, household tape, and more. I was working in their data center, writing computer code. Their term for this was "e-business." It seems quaint now since almost everything is e-business by definition.

I was grateful for the opportunity to work with a large company. However, I didn't feel like my true path was computer engineering or the IT systems space. It took me thirty minutes to walk from my car to my desk! I wasn't convinced the "big company" pathway was for me. My Dad was a salesperson, and I grew up looking up to him. He said, "Why don't you see if you can get a sales internship? I'm sure you'd be great at it."

I went to the sales department as an intern and said, "Look, I haven't done anything other than start a computer networking company. I like talking to people and think I have a good personality for sales."

They said, "That's great, Adam. Why don't you take this thing called the Chally test?"

The Chally test is a career placement exam given by human resource (HR) people. It's still in use today. They ask you a series of questions based on your personality, strengths, and decision-making skills, and the results are matched against their top people. If you pass the test, it means that you are similar to the people who have excelled at their company.

When I discovered I didn't pass the test, I asked for the data so I could figure out why. I was disappointed when they said, "We can't share the data. It's very private." The whole experience felt extremely impersonal. I still think the test itself was faulty because I later moved to California, got involved in sales, and have had a great career both in sales and as a sales consultant.

The inhuman test process I experienced as a young intern was incredibly disheartening. It didn't discourage me from pursuing my goals in sales. But it so easily could have if I had paid attention to the test results and given up.

What I experienced on a small scale is what people, in general, have been experiencing in business on a large scale over the last couple of decades. We've seen a gradual shift toward impersonal, data-driven decision-making and interaction. To understand the dynamics at work and how we arrived at such a place, let's take a quick tour through business history to see the forces that have shaped how we work.

Business is the Story of Technology

We can tell the story of technology in many different ways. We can look at it from the angles of finance, geography, politics, sociology, or systems of commerce, just to name a few. But for our purposes here, I'm going to focus on technology. At its heart, business is the story of technology and how we have invented, used, and advanced it in all its forms.

Today, the word *technology* is often associated with Silicon Valley companies. I prefer to think of it as any means to drive competitive differentiation using the resources available to you. For example, when humans started extracting metal out of the earth, that enabled new types of weapons technology. This naturally gave certain groups a competitive (and deadly) advantage over other groups.

In addition to technology based on materials, there is also *people* technology. This is our way of deploying human resources to differentiate ourselves (or our company or group) from others. All types of technologies can be copied, and that's where culture plays a key role. Business leaders who build technologies based on a culture that embraces creativity and adaptability are much harder to copy.

One of the first major businesses that made efficient use of culture and technology was the Dutch West Indies Company, which brought a culture of tolerance and leniency to the New World. You could be any race or religion and still prosper because they combined their *technology* in human resources in an egalitarian way that promoted individualism, property rights for all, and meritocracy. This happened at a time when most of the land was ruled in the European feudal system, where you were born into wealth. If you weren't one of these lucky few, you'd probably never have wealth.

The Dutch system moved beyond people technology into a new system of government, which is called capitalism today. Even after the English took over New Amsterdam and renamed it New York, they knew this port city on the lower tip of Manhattan not only worked despite its chaos but thrived because of it. That modern approach stayed in New York and spread out across the English colonies in America and eventually the world.

American business exploded over the next couple hundred years, along with innovation, technology, and commerce. By the first half of the twentieth century, the agricultural and industrial revolutions propelled the United States into such success that it became the dominant economy in the world. It had fully evolved into the modern model of skyscrapers and people commuting to work and living in the suburbs, beginning in the postwar 1940s era. The TV show *Mad Men* portrays this era perfectly, with a group of guys working in an office, wearing suits, and doing their best to conquer the world.

It may seem cool from a pop culture perspective, but in truth, it was a very inefficient business model, particularly to shareholders. With each passing decade and each iteration of business, it became more corporate and less personal.

The Era of Optimization and Consolidation

Once the Industrial Revolution had created sweeping changes in every area of business, the early twentieth century saw the roots of modern management begin to take shape. The era of scientific management was sparked by thinkers like Frederick Taylor (1856-1919), the father of modern scientific management. He created the modern hierarchy we see in business structures and is credited with inventing the word "manager." Taylor advocated for productivity and efficiency and felt that employees should operate basically like machines. He also advocated for the division of labor, breaking down pieces of a task into smaller parts that could be performed more efficiently by people doing the same small task over and over again.

By the 1970s and 1980s, business was in full "optimization mode." The most successful companies were the ones able to adopt mathematical modeling and statistical analysis to help make business decisions. Linear programming was widely used for optimizing resource allocation, and you saw the rise of conglomerates made up of other companies.

The best example was General Electric (GE), which saw incredible success due to the business acumen of its legendary Chairman and CEO, Jack Welch, who ran the company in the 1980s and 1990s. He was so powerful that you could almost divide business history into pre-Jack Welch and post-Jack Welch eras.

Much of this was spawned by a notion of Economic Value Added (EVA), which is a financial formula measuring the wealth a company creates. When a company measures its success by this metric, every decision is determined by whether it helps drive the price share forward and optimize the company financially.

This decision-making matrix can get very granular as well as impersonal. For example, when the driving metric of a company is making everything profitable, that determines whether you might use a pen or a pencil on a given day. The factors that drive profit become more important than the humans actually doing the work.

Another type of optimization focused on manufacturing and supply chains. This was called "Six Sigma," which is concerned with reducing the amount of waste in a given process. We were no longer going to build a bunch of stuff, put it in a warehouse, and hope customers bought it. Pioneered by Toyota, we were now going to focus on getting lean and doing *just-in-time* (JIT) manufacturing, optimizing our processes, and trying to eliminate as many defects as possible.

While these optimization methods led to more efficient business operations, they also made jobs more rigid, siloed, and structured, potentially reducing the scope for creativity and autonomy. The trend continues with HR leading us down a data-driven future where we literally view *humans as resources* to be optimized.

We all know that data plays a big role in business today—*perhaps the* primary role. But it's not as if data didn't play a role in business in the 1980s, 1990s, and early 2000s. It just wasn't the primary focus. Everyone was obsessed with optimizing processes and profitability. This model might be well and good until a global pandemic comes along to destroy all predictability in supply chain issues and disrupt manufacturing.

Driven by Data

This brings us to today. I would call this the era of data optimization, or *dataism.* We use data to help us decide where to spend our money, how we should support our customers, how to manage people, and much more.

We all know about companies such as Google and Meta (which owns Facebook) using algorithms and harvesting data to control our attention, then monetizing that attention through advertising. These algorithms are designed to addict us so we never leave the platforms. I remember when websites had a break at the end of a page. Now, everything is an "infinite scroll," which makes it harder to leave.

Back in the 1980s and 1990s, if you weren't able to capture greater financial optimization or increase leniency in your supply chain, you were in a tough spot. Now, we have to focus on decision optimization. If you have the right data on employees or customers, you can better decide where you should spend your money.

How much should I spend on customer support? Should I pair customers in different ways? How should I manage and coach people? Those are significant concerns, and data can help with those decisions. However, just like financial optimization and Six Sigma took the culture and lifeblood out of a company at times, an obsession with data can also do that.

This is why Business Artists are so important. We must never lose the human element in business. We can't get focused on a scientific approach to everything because science can never replace human intuition, creativity, and relationships.

If we go back to the metaphor of music, think about what it takes to create a song. You might start with a base pattern. Then, you'll add some melody and maybe other layers, instruments, or elements. You'll also add some vocals. Yet you can also do it a hundred different ways in all sorts of styles or genres.

This is why we often discover and re-discover the same albums and songs by the same artists over and over. You can hear Bruce Springsteen sing "Glory Days" in a studio version, a live concert version, or a stripped-down Broadway show version. You can get Taylor Swift's album *Midnights* in the original edition or the *Midnights (3am Edition)*. You can get most of the Beatles' albums in various re-released, remastered, and re-issued editions.

These days, there's never just one way to experience an artist's music. You have your pick of digital, vinyl, or CD. That's a good analogy for how business should work. There ought to be various ways to express our creativity in the realm of business in a way that best suits the customer or client experience.

Things don't work as well when you try to put a linear, overly prescriptive experience in place of human processes. That's the source of the resistance we feel in the marketplace today. Everyone has a playbook—a prescribed strategy for accomplishing their goals.

You're probably familiar with a *sales playbook*, a black-and-white, step-by-step process that shows you what to do at every stage of the sales cycle. It begins at point A, progresses to point B, arrives at point C, concludes with a sale at point D, and so on. We have tried to systemize processes for human performance, but it doesn't work because you can't systematize sales any more than you can systematize art.

What would have happened if Miles Davis had gone into the studio and followed the *jazz playbook*? We would have been robbed of

Kind of Blue, one of the greatest albums of all time. He didn't follow a playbook. He followed his humanity and creative spirit.

Sales and business are no different. Just like jazz, there are boundaries, themes, and motifs. What makes jazz "jazz" is when the musician goes outside those boundaries and gives us something fresh and unexpected. But they keep returning to the same motif over and over again in the song.

That's jazz. That's humanity. That's business. If we only operate by a rigid playbook, we risk losing everything meaningful about business.

The Perils of Dataism

Let's dive into the dangers of the world we currently face a little more. Why is this reliance—this obsession, really—on data so dangerous?

Dataism can be a cycle where you become more of who you are against your own will. Getting caught in an algorithm can make you question your identity. From a marketing perspective, the goal of that data is to help make an archetype of you, to serve you ads in your category. You may have heard the term "segment of one," which means that we're going to hyper-personalize our marketing not just to people like you but to you individually. It's a highly efficient use of data, but I would argue that we need to limit it because you don't realize how controlled you are as a customer.

We need to be cautious because trying to perfect everything can become an obsession. We initially used data in advertising, and soon, businesses started focusing on using data to improve everything. This is where data-centric *sales playbook* strategies falter.

For example, the book *The Challenger Sale* uses extensive data to suggest that the best salespeople are *challengers* and recommend that everyone adopt this style. However, this aggressive style can upset customers and neglect the importance of building long-lasting relationships and a more advisory approach. Most importantly, each salesperson has unique talents that, when utilized correctly, can lead to personal satisfaction, higher motivation, and happier customers.

Right before our eyes, we are seeing the logical result of data obsession. Four companies—Apple, Google, Amazon, and Meta (Facebook)—have an outsized influence on society. Are they useful? Of course. Many of us use those companies' products and services on a daily basis. But personalization is not all it's cracked up to be.

Take books, for example. Is Amazon useful because it recommends books and creates a customer experience that can't be rivaled anywhere else online? Yes. But what about the curiosity factor? On Amazon, you can't duplicate the experience of roaming in a bookstore and coming across random titles that can enlighten your mind. Personalization suppresses exploration and discovery. It comes with a price tag, which is living in an echo chamber where data and technology only serve you things you already like and want.

Look no further than Spotify's Discover Weekly feature. It's meant to help you discover new music, but it's really just playing 99 percent of the same music you are already listening to. In the face of algorithms that reflect our images back at us, it's harder and harder to break free and embark on a journey of discovery.

The technology behind the companies that use these vast amounts of data also places too much power into the hands of a few people. History has shown us that it's very hard to use extraordinary amounts of power for the good of society. A nineteenth-century British politician named Lord Acton once wisely said, "Absolute power corrupts absolutely." Today, a half-dozen business tech leaders have an astounding amount of control over society.

Today's Realities and Tomorrow's Challenges

Where does that leave us? Let me wrap up this chapter with a few thoughts.

To put it bluntly, we are increasingly at the mercy of technology and algorithms. These days, every company is a tech company: EdTech, FinTech, AgriTech, PharmaTech, BioTech, and so on. It doesn't matter what industry it is. At its heart, every company has a *tech* heartbeat, whether tech is used in creating new products or in how we deploy them.

In the past, technology was concerned with using resources to drive competitive differentiation. Today, technology is focused on data and human performance, using the tools of code and algorithms.

A good journalist *follows the story*. If we follow the data story, we'll learn that data has gone from letting algorithms help us get across town using GPS, to controlling us to the point of being completely lost without it. Think of the person who uses Google Maps to drive two blocks away rather than using their own sense of direction and common sense.

Our lives are controlled by code and data. We may not see it, but it regulates our behavior in ways we don't even realize, and it has the power to do this even more. This isn't a rant against technology. It has played a beautiful role in driving human efficiency. But when we become servants of it, rather than thinking for ourselves, we lose our sense of identity. With fewer humans doing more of the thinking, we will struggle as a society to grow and innovate as we become passive consumers rather than creators.

On a broader cultural scale (or perhaps we should say a worldwide scale), we have to ask what happens when computers push humans out of the job market and create an entire class of people who no longer contribute to society. All you have to do is look at the current capabilities of AI to see how irrelevant many existing jobs will become in the near future.

To take it a step further, what will happen to democracy when all the social media platforms and big tech companies begin to know our preferences better than we know them ourselves? It may sound far-fetched, but it's not. The implications of the technology that already exists are frightening at best.

What will happen when we rely too heavily on sales and business dashboards to manage people, to have coaching conversations, and to grow and develop talent? Leadership and business success require us to understand the nuances in a way that the coding algorithms cannot always account for. Everything in code was at one point developed by a human being. Even when we add machine learning, where computers write their own instructions, there are flaws in the way we program the computer.

Computers, data, and algorithms cannot duplicate human intuition. If we keep moving on the same path, we will lose the elements of culture and business that make us human. The Business Artist will eventually become extinct, relegated to the footnotes of business history books.

Shortly after the COVID-19 restrictions began to lift, DJ Paoni, the CEO of SAP North America, told me, "I'm encouraging all of my sales teams to get back on airplanes to visit customers face to face. Not because I think it's necessary for sustaining our relationships, but because I think it's necessary for them to get their mojo and energy back, to listen and learn from the world and not fall into the trap I'm seeing where many think they can just live behind a desk now and be fulfilled."

He hit the nail on the head. If things remain unchanged, we're headed for a reality where no one will be fulfilled, and Business Artists no longer have a voice. We've arrived at a place where business seems dissonant and out of tune because we've become obsessed with data and algorithms. This has led to three specific problems we'll explore in the next few chapters: problems of *imitation, perception,* and *automation.*

2

THE COVER BAND SYNDROME (AN IMITATION PROBLEM)

Ever since Steve Jobs introduced the iPhone in 2007, smartphones have radically changed our lives. The ways we communicate, entertain ourselves, send email, and even pay for things are vastly different than they were back then.

One of the less obvious ways smartphones have impacted our lives is that they've taught us new ways to get to the same place. Even if you've driven the same way to work for the last ten years, GPS can show you several other ways to get there.

But take a look at human nature for a moment. Even when you know there might be a better or more effective way to do something, you still end up going the same way you've always gone. A routine gives you comfort and reduces stress. You fill your days with habits and actions designed to reduce friction and make life easier. It's much easier to do what you've always done, even when you know there's a better way.

It's Not Enough to Be a Cover Band

The tendency to do what we've always done is not just true in navigation or the habits of our daily lives. It's true in business as well.

Most people follow current systems and processes because it's frustrating to try something new. It requires time and experimentation, not to mention the willingness to get a little lost. You may even have to show a proof of concept to your company to get permission to move forward. But if you work at a company that rewards, or at least tolerates, creativity and innovation, it can be incredibly fulfilling to change your processes.

As a Business Artist, you must give yourself permission to change. Don't just imitate what others are doing. Instead, choose to create. But keep in mind that the creative process, by its very definition of initiating change, requires you to let go of the need to ask for permission.

Let me ask you: Are you willing to try new things? To experiment? To boldly take action and take a risk because you didn't ask for permission?

During the pandemic, I did a lot of experiments to make sure we delivered and scaled virtually in ways that worked. I wanted to try out some new ways to engage customers, given the fact that they were going through the pandemic as well. Maybe, just like me, they didn't want to sit on Zoom calls all day long.

I outfitted my home in LA with multiple cameras, a tripod, and a green screen, and I downloaded some video editing software. I started experimenting and making video proposals that had some flair. On the screen, I used overlaid images and added some moving objects.

It took a little time to get the process going, but eventually, I made them faster than I could make presentation slides. Clients loved the videos! Several of my colleagues were intrigued. Everybody wanted to know how I did it, what my system was, and what software I used. I wanted to help them succeed, so I trained them to use my system.

I learned something interesting in this process: I could teach people to mimic my process and style, but that wasn't my goal. I wanted them to take the basic system and adapt it to their personalities to find their own style. A few of them started to go down this road, but others struggled to inject their personalities into the process.

The whole experience was a reminder that even when you're trying to teach people to be creative, there's always a tendency for them to just copy what they know instead of adapting it to their personal context.

A key principle of *The Business Artist* philosophy is experimenting with artistic creativity. It's all about making connections, seeing patterns where others do not, and expressing thoughts and emotions in a unique way.

This is a microcosm of the larger problem we face in business today: the problem of *imitation*. It's so much easier to just copy what another business or leader is doing rather than think for ourselves. At its core, it's not just a business problem—it's a *human* problem. Left to our own devices, we take the path of least resistance and search for the most painless way to get things done.

Much of the time, businesses are run like they're cover bands. A cover band can mimic the original artist's sound and style, but they don't create anything new. It's a carbon copy of the original. It has the essence, but it's slightly degraded with each subsequent generated copy, like a cassette recording that's been dubbed a few too many times.

Cover bands have their place in society. They're great for entertainment but not for creating anything new. But for Business Artists, it's not enough to just operate as a faint copy of someone else. True Business Artists want to do more than just follow a script or mimic outdated sales and business practices.

The *cover band syndrome* is not just limited to individuals. It also happens to lots of companies. No company is immune from becoming a shadow of its former self, even if it's making more money than ever.

And even if it's the biggest company in the world.

Apple: The World's Biggest Cover Band

I know Apple has a lot of fanboys and fangirls. If you're one of them or even just a casual Apple user, I want to make it clear that I have immense respect for what Steve Jobs and so many others have built over the last few decades.

But please, hear me out.

Apple used to be the very definition of innovation. To put it in music terms, Apple went platinum on almost every album for decades, but now they can't seem to get on a Billboard chart with even one song anymore. People used to queue in front of the stores for new product releases. It was a sold-out show every time.

It's not that Apple doesn't innovate anymore. It's just that their innovation cycles are slower and less effective. They used to have a culture of creativity. Any idea from anyone in the company was welcome. They were constantly ahead of the market, even creating new markets in the process.

If you look back on the history of Apple, the company was first in lots of categories:

- The first to revolutionize the home PC market

- The first to bring artists' entire music catalogs to a mobile device (the iPod)

- The first to build a digital marketplace for music (iTunes)

- The first to combine a phone, music, and the internet all into one device (the iPhone, which created a whole new category of device)

- The first to build a robust marketplace that seamlessly blended developers and mobile devices (the App Store)

- The first to find the hybrid sweet spot of desktop and mobile (the iPad)

- The first to popularize a smart wearable device (the Apple Watch)

The Apple team was a group of visionaries who didn't wonder, *What is the market doing that we could do better?* Instead, they wanted to find what the market wasn't doing and what people needed. Then, they experimented, failed forward, and built products and ideas that drove the market ahead in a profound way. In the process, they usually created an entirely new market that other companies used to launch their own products.

Today, Apple is stuck in an endless cycle of imitating its past success. It's a "legacy band" playing its old hits for crowds, sucking as much revenue and profit from those hits with incremental hardware and software updates. They make decisions to maximize short-term shareholder returns instead of investing time, money, and energy into long-term markets and improving innovation.

I can already hear the objections. "But what about Apple's new Vision Pro headset? That looks incredibly innovative!" True, it does look like a lot of fun! But mixed reality headsets, especially ones like Vision Pro, which retails for $3,499, will probably not rise to the level of an *essential product*. It is an amazingly disruptive product, maybe ahead of its time, like the Tesla Roadster.

Let me be fair, though. To Apple's enduring credit, the company has continued to perform well financially. It's one of the most valuable company in the world. But because of its success, the company is more focused on maintaining what it's built rather than truly innovating.

It's easy to look back at the years when Steve Jobs ran the company and see them through rose-colored glasses. In many ways, they were indeed the golden years of Apple. But remember, Steve didn't always get it right. In 2007, he famously decreed, "People want to own their music." He should have been looking forward to the innovation of streaming music instead of owning it. Apple eventually became a me-too follower of Spotify, which had the dominant algorithm and biggest catalog of artists.

There's a great lesson here for every Business Artist. You can become so successful that you box yourself into a corner. Then, you become a legacy company in the vein of Coca-Cola, which has successfully sold the same basic product for well over one hundred years.

There's nothing wrong with being profitable. But we should never confuse profitability with innovation.

The Path of Least Resistance

It's easy to point fingers at Apple since they're the "big dog," and everybody knows the company's story. It's harder to take a long, honest look at yourself in the mirror and ask whether you would do the same thing in their shoes. Is it possible for you and me to become cover bands of ourselves, simply imitating our past success and continuing to churn out tired renditions of the same old songs?

The answer is "yes." That's what the vast majority of us do unless we take pains to change course. Perhaps it's helpful to look at why we tend to give up on innovation. Why do we usually resort to the path of least resistance not only in business—but also in life?

That's a big question with probably even bigger answers, but let me take a stab at it. As we discussed in the book's introduction, we consume more than we create. When that happens, we operate from a place of judgment of other people's creations and limit ourselves by starving our artistic sensibilities.

As a result, we seek out safe ways to find meager success instead of learning through failure. When you come from a place of judgment and always find fault with others, you avoid the risk of failure at any cost. But if you operate from a place of generosity and creativity, it's much easier to take a risk because you don't see *failure* as the final word.

In fact, you don't see *failure* at all because you reframe every failure as an opportunity to learn and improve.

When I was in business school at USC, the leader of Fox Filmed Entertainment made a fascinating statement. He said, "Most of the time, we look for the least risky projects. We don't make big bets often. Instead, we wait and see what is working, and then we do that."

That mentality is why you see so many sequels and comic book movies today. They already have a built-in audience. It costs a lot of money to take a risk and produce something new and unique.

Let's put this in terms of sales. I often see enablement teams as the problem, not the sellers. There is a temptation to create accreditation programs for everything from making a discovery call, selling against your competition, or delivering an elevator pitch for a product. In most cases, sellers end up memorizing a script that doesn't jive with their style. They get *certified* and are expected to use this approach in customer conversations.

The only problem is that each customer interaction is a bit different. People are individuals. Each person comes from their own unique perspective and set of needs. When salespeople rely on an overly rigid one-size-fits-all approach, it doesn't work.

We can also look at this from a more basic biological perspective. Human beings generally take the path of least resistance since it requires less thinking. Thinking requires energy, and like all land mammals, we are programmed to preserve energy. It's not that we're lazy. It's that we have adapted to having a large prefrontal cortex. This is the part of our brain that recognizes patterns and operates with more reason than the part of our brain that purely reacts.

We even have lactic acid buildup in our muscles from the evolutionary process to tell us when our muscles are fatigued and we're done. We can push through this barrier, but it is very difficult to go against our bio-engineering.

The same is true for our brains. We are wired to find the fastest way to an outcome. Over millions of years, our neurons have evolved pattern recognition that makes it difficult to break this cycle even if we want to.

Knowing all this, how can we still maintain a sense of innovation and creativity? How do we press forward as Business Artists despite our biological tendency to seek out the easiest path? There are perhaps many answers, but one of them is to find inspiration in companies that broke the mold of their industry and didn't settle for the status quo.

Netflix: From Outlier to Industry Leader

The term *status quo* comes from Latin and literally means *the existing state of affairs*. Companies that challenge the existing state of affairs are not content with the current scenario. Instead, they want to disrupt the current state of affairs and create a new reality. They have the courage to ask, "What if things were different?"

That's exactly what Netflix did. Although Netflix might be *old hat* by now since it's been around a long time (at least in terms of streaming services), it didn't start out that way. The company began in 1998 as an online DVD rental service. Who else remembers the days when Netflix would deliver DVDs to your mailbox in those red envelopes? (And no late fees!)

In its early days, Netflix hosted a contest to build its machine-learning algorithm to recommend movies to users. They were getting it wrong with customers, and their data scientists could not figure out the correct algorithm to produce the best results.

The CEO turned to external sources and launched a $10 million dollar contest. Think about this for a moment. In the world of data, movies are tough to nail down. Just because someone gives a movie five stars doesn't mean they actually enjoyed it. If you rate *Schindler's List* as a five-star movie, you might be saying, "I want to like this," instead of indicating you actually enjoyed it.

As a result of the contest, a brilliant college student was awarded millions of dollars for coming up with the algorithm Netflix now uses. His basic argument was that people lie unconditionally about what they say they like when it comes to entertainment. The logic was, "Let's stop believing how they rate movies and instead look at their browsing history, their Instagram activity, their buying behavior, their social status, their income, and other factors. And let's use that to see if we can't predict more accurately what movies they'd like."

If two people set up a Netflix account today and watched the same ten movies or TV shows, and they rated them all the same, Netflix would recommend different items to them. This fascinating study reminds us of an uncomfortable truth: Don't believe what your customer says but instead look at their actual behavior.

Netflix didn't become an industry leader by imitating other companies. Netflix chose to do something totally different, initially becoming an outlier, then eventually becoming the leader others imitated.

This is our goal with Meahana. Our mission is to unlock the inner facilitator in everyone and celebrate innovation rather than mere imitation. We provide sophisticated yet user-friendly tools that foster originality and collaboration while enabling professionals to learn and connect in exciting ways. And with the evolution of work dynamics due to technology, we encourage adaptability, an essential aspect of The Business Artist philosophy.

You don't have to be Netflix to make a difference in your industry. You just have to choose to be different in the first place.

The Biggest Danger is Imitating Yourself

If you're reading this book, you probably want to do everything in your power to avoid imitating others or, worse, your past success.

There's a simple reason why it's hard to do this. The most popular leaders, bands, or entertainers are those who keep doing the same things over and over again. The biggest legacy acts today—Billy Joel, Bruce Springsteen, Paul McCartney, Journey, and a handful of others—make a great living not by forging new creative pathways, but by playing the same decades-old hits.

It's strange but true: Success can be one of the worst things to happen to artists' creativity, especially in their younger years. Just ask the cast members of massively successful TV hits like *Friends* or *Seinfeld*. Except for Jerry Seinfeld, Julia Louis-Dreyfus (both of *Seinfeld*), and

Jennifer Aniston (of *Friends*), none of the cast members found long-term success after their hit TV shows.

Why? Because they were forever tied to those characters. It was impossible for them to escape those personas, even though all of them were massively talented. Case in point: Jason Alexander (who played George on *Seinfeld*) is a gifted dramatic actor who came from the world of theater when he auditioned for Seinfeld. But he will forever be tied to the role of George Costanza.

For many of the world's greatest artists, no matter their medium, their greatest enemy is not a lack of opportunity, studios, record labels, or agents. Their greatest enemy is their past success. It's like fighting a shadow version of yourself.

It's not just big-time music acts or sitcom stars who are prone to the dangers of the cover band syndrome. We all are.

In my sales consulting career, where my client needs change quickly, I can think of at least two times when I sold something that was quick but missed the mark in terms of what they needed. I fell victim to imitating myself. Since these clients knew me and my previous success with other clients, they were almost pressuring me to imitate myself and my past solution for them. Rather than challenging them, I went along.

Other times, I've found myself making a quick sale that may have been easy (because I'm good at sales and storytelling), but I missed the mark on what the customer really needed. The client said something that reminded me of another client project that I worked on, and I fell victim to assuming their needs were the same instead of taking the time to truly listen and ensure I was giving them the best solution.

In business, we spend a good amount of time paying attention to our competitors, wondering if we're keeping up, or what they might have up their sleeves next. It's important to keep a competitive advantage, to be sure, but the biggest enemy is not out there. It's the one staring back at us in the mirror.

To make matters even more pressing, the cover band syndrome is only one of three critical problems we're looking at here in Part 1. Now, we turn our attention to the second one: the problem of perception.

3

THE CHASM BETWEEN ART AND BUSINESS (A PERCEPTION PROBLEM)

We humans have a natural tendency to draw borders. We like to know who's *in* and *out* of our tribes. This tendency to categorize people and define the boundaries of our social group is baked into our very DNA.

We carry this tendency into every sphere of our lives, including business and the arts. In Western culture, we see business and art as mostly separate pursuits. We picture a typical businessperson as a buttoned-up CEO type who keeps a rigid nine-to-five schedule at the office. On the other hand, we picture the typical artist as a free-thinking spirit with no discipline and little understanding of how business works.

These tropes have been perpetuated for hundreds of years but are not always true. If I look at my social network of friends and colleagues, almost all of them do some kind of creative work in their social lives.

It might be playing an instrument, cooking at home, making school projects with their kids, or a dozen other things. They aren't following a recipe. Instead, they're experimenting, ideating, scrapping the first idea, and moving on to another. They're artists.

I believe that's true for most people. Even if we have a very *business-y* job, we still have creative pursuits in our lives. Whether creating a work of art, an experience, or a slide deck, we have artistic choices available to us that will impact the result. It's important to pay attention to the creative elements in everything we do.

We're all mostly making this up as we go along. We're all playing jazz. We're all Business Artists finding our way, sometimes without a clear map to guide us.

Maps can be great, but many of us operate in roles or jobs where there's no map at all. Over the last few years, the world has changed drastically. We have the maps from the past, but we have to draw new maps because the ones we're using are outdated or inaccurate. They no longer describe the terrain in front of us.

If we're going to navigate this new, complex world, we need to first understand more about the historical great divide between business and the arts.

The Great Divide

As I mentioned, most people in business have some degree of creativity in their personal lives. Yet, most business leaders still believe that business should be driven by logic, reason, and linear thinking. They don't see the need for creative thinking and new solutions, even though the most successful companies thrive because of innovation.

To put it another way, many business leaders want innovation, but they don't see that a company culture of creative thinking is needed to make innovation possible. They downplay activities that don't seem based on logic and reason.

For example, you can't *do innovation* in a thirty-minute Zoom meeting, or perhaps not virtually at all. From a sales perspective, you can't teach people how to be Business Artists with a *framework*. It goes against the very nature of what it means to be an artist who uniquely expresses themselves. You can't teach someone how to innovate exactly as you do.

Your approach to business is like a fingerprint. It's unique to you. You don't share it with anyone else in the world. Everyone has a fingerprint (ten of them, to be exact!), but no two peoples' fingerprints are exactly the same.

In business today, there's a great divide between people who understand the role that creative thinking and company culture plays in innovation, and those who don't. That's why it's vital for every leader to understand how creative people think.

Learning to Think Like an Artist

One of my favorite storytelling moments has no dialogue.

In the first three minutes of the Disney Pixar movie *UP*, you learn about the main character, his background, his personality, his struggles, his wants and dreams, and his purpose. All of these scenes were artistic choices meant to paint a narrative and give the audience understanding. And it all takes place without a word being spoken.

Likewise, if you've seen the movie *Joker*, starring Joaquin Phoenix, you'll remember that the first scenes show him walking up a staircase at his apartment and getting bumped into by neighbors who do not notice him. The music cuts out every time he opens his mailbox and sees nothing inside. Then *clash*, you hear the sound of an empty mailbox shutting.

A normal person today might say, "Wow, that is a super slow intro. Let's get to the car chase or whatever else a Marvel movie would have done by now." But in this movie, director Todd Phillips used a set of artistic choices to make the audience understand how this character feels alone and invisible.

Joker was a huge box-office success not only because of the compelling origin story of the main character but because of the many thousands of artistic choices made by the director, cast, crew, and others who worked on the film.

Sometimes, we see a great work of art and think to ourselves, *I could never do that.* But remember, those creative choices are available to you as well. If you start paying attention to art, you can begin to use its power in how you communicate in a sales environment. What artistic choices do you have at your disposal to alter the way someone will interpret your message? How can you, as a Business Artist, start to experiment to see what works for you?

One of my former BTS colleagues, Peter Mulford, is a great example of what we're talking about. (BTS is a global strategy implementation consulting firm and my former employer.) Peter created what you might call a new form of music for our customers and internal stakeholders to inspire them and help develop new ideas. He named it the Innovation and Digital Transformation (IDX) practice. He cross-pollinates these IDX tools and principles into other parts of the business, including sales.

While they use design thinking and other innovation principles with clients, they also would lead the way in how we, as a consulting firm, should operate internally and how to get the most out of each group or individual.

Peter uses a concept called *idea flow,* which, for him, involves getting as much input from different parts of the business as possible to tackle the main problem. It's essentially quantity over quality— divergent thinking before convergent thinking. All the solutions he enables the team to build are far more innovative than any one person would come up with.

Surprisingly, there are no politics involved in ownership. It's a beautiful thing. The end set of ideas is inspired by this practice of exploration and widening the scope and diversity of input in an artful manner.

I would call Peter the poster child at BTS in terms of being a Business Artist who brings new creative ideas to life and is constantly experimenting with new methods. In any new process, he involves other people to add even more value. It's a great template for good enterprise salespeople.

If you look at most successful salespeople, they don't use boilerplate marketing language for their products. They go wide to listen to other ideas and to better understand customer perception. They find their competitive edge in the marketplace and then double down on it. They also use recent earnings statements, primary quotes, and other research to make their proposals contextual and customized to the audience.

One of the reasons Peter is so successful is that he comes to his work with a creating, rather than a possessing, mindset. He gets as much input from as many different parts of the business as possible. Peter is one of the most generous and unselfish people I know. This quality is what allows him to draw out the best from the people around him.

Three Core Principles for Business Artists

As you can tell, I'm not a big fan of rigid guidelines. There are exceptions to almost every rule. However, it will be helpful to share three core principles that describe how Business Artists think and work. These principles are a compass that can help you understand the value you add to your business and to society as a whole.

1. **Creativity and Innovation**. Picture a jazz soloist, improvising a melody on the fly. That's the spirit of a Business Artist, blending the specifics of what we sell or do with new ideas and creative thinking. We push boundaries, find novel ideas, and navigate through changes, often turning technology and automation into tools for greater innovation.

2. **Human Connection and Emotional Intelligence**. In jazz, the magic lies in the connection between the musicians, who are all attuned to each other's rhythm. We recognize the diverse strengths each of us brings to the table, and we cultivate a culture of trust, improvisation, and shared accountability. We connect with customers on an emotional level and don't look

at sales as a linear process of handoffs. Instead, we see it as an opportunity to connect and create value.

3. **Adaptability and Continuous Learning**. This is our ability to alter the tempo, to create space and movement to connect the dots forward on new ideas. We dance to the rhythm of change, not just responding to it, but actively embracing it as an opportunity for growth. To avoid being a cover band of our past success, we commit to ongoing education and finding new mistakes to learn from along the way.

These core principles aren't just buzzwords to put on a list or throw onto a social media post. These are the real bread and butter of how artists must operate. It's exciting yet simultaneously a little frustrating.

Why? Because the story of humanity is the perennial struggle between accepting the status quo and choosing to innovate. From the birth of modern humans, we have been hard-wired to avoid innovation. We are programmed to embrace the status quo, whether as hunter-gatherers on prehistoric plains or hunter-gatherers in the modern boardroom.

It's not your fault that innovation feels risky or that it's not accepted in your organization. I've read an enormous amount of leadership literature on how we need to challenge the status quo, think outside the box, or get out of our own *rivers of thinking*.

However, this desire for the status quo is no longer relevant. The convergence of technology, AI, globalization, and other forces means we need to embrace our humanity and work to draw out the creative thinking that lies within each of us.

At its heart, this is a problem of perception. Whereas in Chapter 2, we talked about the problem of imitation, here we are broadening the scope and asking, "Why exactly do we imitate rather than innovate?" One of the major reasons is that we don't see ourselves as particularly creative or capable of implementing new ideas.

This is why music, movies, and the arts are so critical to your development as a businessperson. While it may seem like the latest

Hollywood movie doesn't have anything to do with your sales quota or what happens in the boardroom, they are intimately connected. Every minute you spend engrossed in the arts is a minute you're growing as a creative human being.

A Few Examples of Business Artists

I introduced you to my friend Peter Mulford earlier in the chapter. He personifies the principles of the Business Artist. Let me flesh out these concepts a bit more by sharing some other examples.

We're all familiar with Dr. Dre (founder of Beats by Dre), Jay-Z, Sean Combs, and other musicians who have created business empires. But the concept of the Business Artist can go far beyond that. You don't have to be a painter or a musician. You can work in a high-rise, work from home, or work in hotel rooms while traveling for business. The defining quality of a Business Artist is that you act artistically to fulfill your business role.

It doesn't matter if you're making music, making a presentation, or making sales to customers. Business is all about adding value to others with the exchange of a product or service for money. Each party in a business transaction should come away feeling like they received more value than they gave. That's what makes business, business.

One of my favorite quotes on this topic comes, ironically, from the iconic artist Andy Warhol. He said, "Being good in business is the most fascinating kind of art." He recognizes there is artistry involved in doing business well. It's not just about numbers and profit, but also about creativity, connection, and individual expression. Just like art, good business practices have the power to engage people emotionally.

One of the all-time great Business Artists was the legendary David Bowie. He pushed all sorts of creative and social boundaries during his epic career. His experiments with the music industry and economics may be lesser known, however. In the 1990s, David Bowie created "Bowie Bonds," offering his fans a chance to share in the ownership of his intellectual property. It was a groundbreaking experiment, and Bowie Bonds was part of the inspiration for SingularDTV (a blockchain entertainment studio focusing on creating a decentralized entertainment industry).

In 1996, Bowie was the first artist to sell a song online, receiving more than 300,000 downloads of his tune "Telling Lies." He even launched his own internet service provider in 1998 called BowieNet. Although it wasn't an enduring success, I give him credit for doing something ambitious and unexpected.

Innovation has always been led by artists, whether they are operating on stage or in a more traditional business setting. Business Artists cannot be constricted by roles, titles, or the conventions that society places on them. They are always experimenting and testing to see what sticks.

At this point, you may be wondering, *Adam, this all sounds well and good. I love your perspective and want to be a more effective Business Artist. But how do I balance the creative side of things with the needs and demands of a fast-paced business with customers, schedules, inventory, and other traditional elements of business? How do I keep a balance between the passion for creativity and the process of business?*

Let's explore this tension and find some ways that we can move beyond ignoring it and instead learn to embrace and celebrate it.

The Tension Between Passion and Process

The ideas we've talked about in the book so far are helpful, perhaps even revolutionary in some ways. But the question remains: How do you put these concepts into practice in the real world? How can you be creative and nimble, but also value and respect the processes of business?

The answer is that it's not an either-or thing. You need them both. If you only have passion with no guidelines, parameters, or processes, you end up with half-finished projects and creative energy leading to ideas that don't go anywhere. If you only have processes, you'll have all the efficiency in the world but no creative spark to breathe life into your work.

You can see a good example of process without passion in many high-growth tech companies today. There is too much reliance on templates for everything from sales decks to marketing communications and everything else. I understand that you need to save time, but in the long run, you end up having sellers who send the same deck to customers with very different needs.

When you have a process that requires you to use a template or start with a re-use deck, it snatches away the natural creativity that could make the sales process something truly special and perhaps even fun again!

Anytime there's a new process in place, it should be implemented with a set of guidelines that still allow passionate individuals to operate with some creative autonomy in the right areas. In the world of sales, I've seen a number of processes put in place during a transformation that, on the surface, was meant to help the organization scale and grow. However, they sucked the passion and human touch out of the business.

A simple sales phone call or email has now been replaced by an excessively analytical intake form or a rigorous approval process. Salespeople who have worked tirelessly to engage a customer find themselves grappling with a convoluted approval process, often humorously referred to as answering to the *revenue police*.

Or you might have a situation where the company has introduced a new sales methodology or a sales process based on how much you're charging or how you're selling. If they have co-created this with people in the field, Business Artists may like it because they've had input. But more often, they get off-the-shelf sales training.

Salespeople do not all sell the same way. We'd never expect every CEO to lead the same way or every consultant to take the exact same approach. Yet, in the business world, we've spent untold amounts of time, energy, money, and human capital trying to perfect the perfect sales approach, all while totally forgetting that people are individuals who want to have some leeway in how they achieve their sales goals.

For salespeople, it's about being creative and artistic in the way you show up in front of customers and your teams.

Another example: What about customer relationship management (CRMs) and the way they are usually introduced in a company? Takes Salesforce, the most prominent CRM. It's not typically sold to a salesperson in the field. It's sold to a sales leader within the company. The sales leader wants visibility. They want to see where the sales activity is happening, and they want to be able to forecast.

Those aren't bad goals, but salespeople don't have those concerns about what their colleagues are doing or what the quarterly sales forecast needs to be. They are worried mainly about their own sales.

The sellers should be able to find a lot of value in this system. Yet, they are often forced to work with a version of a CRM that was not designed primarily for them and doesn't have the flexibility to adapt. This makes it feel like a compliance activity they are obligated to use rather than feeling motivated.

Imagine if recording artists had their record label choose the instruments they had to use when making an album. We would lose the evolution and creativity we hear in music today. It's a classic case of the tail wagging the dog.

This kind of approach diminishes the talents of salespeople and moves them further away from being Business Artists. When they are constrained by the system rather than being freed by it, everyone suffers.

As it turns out, CRMs may be the least of our worries as we continue to see the stunning rise of automation in every facet of modern life. Now that we've taken a look at an imitation problem in Chapter 2, and a perception problem here in Chapter 3, in Chapter 4, we'll look at the problem of automation, which has taken on a new sense of urgency in recent years.

4

HUMANS VS. ALGORITHMS (AN AUTOMATION PROBLEM)

Star Trek is one of the most enduring pop culture franchises of all time. Created in the 1960s by the visionary Gene Roddenberry, the franchise's movies and TV shows explore the interplanetary adventures of different crews at different time periods. They generally take place between the twenty-second and twenty-fourth centuries.

That's far enough into the future to imagine technologies that won't exist for some time (or may never exist) but close enough to our time frame that the stories don't seem too far-fetched.

In the 1960s, when the original TV show aired, artificial intelligence (AI) and computers that could perform highly advanced tasks seemed like science fiction. But now we're living in a time when many of the sci-fi tropes of the past have become reality.

Case in point: When you were a kid, did you ever imagine communicating with a robot in the grocery store? Yet today, you can go into many grocery stores in the U.S. and encounter roving robots that scan shelves, dispense coupons, and more. This is only the tip of the iceberg. Robots and AI have become a part of nearly every industry in one form or another.

At this point, we're too dependent on AI and algorithms to stop using them. And would we even want to? Given all our concerns about automation and related developments, it's still pretty convenient to use Amazon Prime shipping or ask your phone to give you directions to a restaurant across town.

Why? Because modern life and business demand that we complete things quickly, efficiently, and reliably. That's why we give more and more tasks to algorithms. That's a convenient way to live—until it isn't.

For example, in 2014, the entire 911 emergency call system went down for six hours. Somewhere in the code, the programmers put an upper limit to the number of calls it would handle. When that limit was reached, it stopped routing calls altogether. Code and algorithms will always begin with humans giving input. In a sense, we have ourselves to blame for any negative consequences of technology.

So far in the book, we've explored a range of issues related to business, creativity, and art. In human history, we've always had the temptation to imitate others instead of producing our own creative work (Chapter 2). Likewise, in Western culture, there has always been a division of sorts between business and the arts (Chapter 3). However, the issues and questions we face related to technology and algorithms are relatively new because they have advanced so quickly in the last few decades.

As we consider how to become better Business Artists, we need to pause and explore our relationship with technology. We have become obsessed with progress, efficiency, and measurement. But is this a good thing? After all, business is a *human* endeavor.

The point of life is to have a human experience, not a technological one. We stand at a crossroads in our development. Over time, humans and technology will be so intertwined that you won't be able to tell where one ends and the other begins.

In other words, we face the problem of *automation*. The place to begin our discussion is not with technology itself but with the most fundamental question of all.

What Does It Mean to Be Human?

As you already know, this isn't really a science or philosophy book. However, it does draw in those elements when needed because I'm attempting to give you a big-picture view we can then use to shed some light on bringing more creativity into the business world. In that sense, it's pretty important to look at this question of "What does it mean to be human?" from different viewpoints.

One of the simplest, most basic ways to define *humans* is that we have the capacity to create and imagine. Can plants and animals change the environment? Of course. But they don't have the ability to form societies that can dominate all other animals.

Humans are also different from computers or machines. Computers can generate information much faster than humans, but only with precise instructions. Technology has always been part of the development process in human culture, but only because technology was first *created* by humans.

One of the defining qualities of human beings is that we have a built-in desire to innovate, not just imitate. When we imitate others, that's acting more like a machine than a human. Computers and machines are designed to follow input and carry out instructions, even if that work is using a generative pre-trained transformer (GPT) to create *original* work.

GPT is like an experienced chef who has tasted many dishes and flavors. It can now imagine and create new recipes from its experience. Keep that phrase in mind: "from its experience." It will not create and experiment with recipes that have never been made before.

It will *create*, but it is not *creative*. AI does not generate novel ideas, connect disparate concepts, or express itself in any original way. It has no intent, is inconsistent, and lacks purpose in its task.

I know it sounds crazy, but you don't have to be *creative* to *create*. AI cannot make mental leaps that lead to legitimate innovation. The real human innovators are the ones who are programming the algorithms or building new tools that can help humans create.

In addition to having the capacity to create, a second defining characteristic of humans is that we live in the tension between collaboration and freedom. One of the basic rights we feel we must have as humans is freedom. Whenever freedom is taken away, our humanity is stripped away. That is what makes slavery such an evil human enterprise. It strips away the most basic, fundamental aspect of who we are as humans: people who are free. The core reason for every war in history is the pursuit of freedom. We will go to great lengths to preserve, protect, and defend it.

Yet, at the same time, we deeply value collaboration, which, in some ways, is a compromise of freedom. When we collaborate, we give up a part of our freedom and autonomy in order to build something greater than we could ever build as individuals.

Collaborating with other humans while also being humane to them is deeply rooted in the human experience. We work together, empathize with each other, and grow together, all while expressing our individual selves. This means recognizing and accepting our weaknesses while leveraging our unique strengths where possible to maximize our fulfillment of self.

It's a constant dance where we juggle the seemingly incompatible values of freedom and collaboration to maximize both. The tension we feel in the creative process comes from needing to adjust one of these elements.

Can Humans Be Automated?

The question above might sound a little crazy. Only machines and computers can be automated, right?

Not so fast. Humans are capable of incredible amounts of repetition and automatic behavior. That can be a good thing or a bad thing, depending on the behavior. Much of the vast amount of habit-building literature is focused on helping people build automatic healthy behaviors that improve their lives.

At the same time, human behavior can be automated in unhealthy or destructive ways. If you use an iPhone, you've probably noticed the weekly "Screen Time" report that shows how much time you have stared at the screen in the previous seven days. You may have also seen reports about how many times a day (dozens!) the average person looks at their phone or how many times they check their email.

What about the person who gets up every morning and just *has* to have a cup of coffee to get the day started? That's automation. Or what about the times when you got into your car and meant to go somewhere besides work, but you still ended up driving in the direction toward work because that's where you've driven for years?

We think of ourselves as free creatures who could never be automated. But our behavior says otherwise. It's not a question of *whether* humans are automated. We are. It's impossible to totally escape automation because we're wired to operate by habits.

The issue, then, is where to draw a line in the sand. What boundaries should we put in place to help ensure we can function at our best as Business Artists? How do we release our full creative powers instead of just becoming automated machines—whether by our own habits or by the automation of algorithms?

Drawing the Boundaries

As far as automation goes, one of the most pressing concerns we are dealing with today is how to think about AI-generated content. For example, you can give AI a prompt such as "Write an article about five ways to be more creative" or "Draw a picture of an astronaut riding a horse in the style of Andy Warhol."

In this case, we are using AI simply as a technology tool, not unlike other digital photography tools and software available today. It's a giant leap forward as far as its capability, and in some ways, it unlocks our creativity. But it's nothing more than a tool, in the same way a car enables you to get somewhere faster. You are still part of the creative process because you are giving it input.

AI can have lots of wonderful uses, including a chatbot experience. You've probably used these on various websites as you've tried to find specific information or get help with billing. AI can be useful in enhancing creativity or communication.

What about when Photoshop was introduced? Nobody complains today that software such as Photoshop is an intrusion on human creativity. It's simply a tool that unlocks more creative potential than was possible before. Now, Photoshop has generative AI fill capabilities to extend creativity. After all, isn't that what technology is supposed to do in the first place—increase our creative potential and help us bring more good into the world?

Where I draw the line is when technology is used to hurt or deceive others. One such area is deepfakes, which is the practice of creating realistic-looking videos of people doing or saying things they didn't do. The whole purpose is to *fake* or deceive. That clearly crosses an ethical line.

Similar technology can be used to de-age characters in movies, many times with stunning results. The question is not, "Is a certain type of technology good or bad?" Instead, it's "How can we use this technology for good purposes and avoid using it for evil?"

Nuclear reactions can be used to decimate an entire city or provide an endless supply of energy to the same people. It's all in how you use it. We could say the same thing about data.

Data is Not Enough

Business works best when it's not just concerned about making money but is also focused on improving communities and the lives of its employees.

The role of data in our modern world should be to inform us, not rule us. This is where AI can do a better job than we can as humans. It can evaluate complex and even emotional data input, filtering out what is and isn't important, learning from other data, and then guiding us. But if you rely solely on data to make decisions, you can use the numbers to justify almost anything if you try hard enough.

For example, every state in the U.S. had access to the exact same COVID-19 data, yet there was a wide array of responses to it. Some states had strict mask policies, others were much looser, and most were somewhere in the middle. Data itself can't make decisions for you. Data doesn't know your context, and it can't lead people. It must always be interpreted, understood, contextualized, and then applied.

One of the responsibilities of a business leader is to sift through disparate, sometimes contradictory, information and make decisions based on instinct, experience, and relationships. You can't take a purely scientific approach when you're dealing with human emotions and shifting global markets.

Data can make us better businesspeople as long as we treat it as a tool and not as gospel.

Much of it has to do with the quality of your data, how much you have, how quick your data processing tools are, and how well you can make a decision that takes data into consideration.

Despite all the reasons to use data and all the good it can do, it's not the only factor in a company's success. The reason is that success doesn't just rely on number-crunching. In an ever-changing world where global forces affect everything and everyone, business leadership requires uniquely human qualities like negotiation, empathy, and courage.

Sometimes, great leadership requires you to go against the data entirely.

Two Examples of Ignoring the Data

Business history is replete with stories of companies that went against the odds and ignored what the data told them, only to find great success. Here are two great examples.

For years, HBO has been known as a company that goes against conventional wisdom, betting on shows that other networks turned down. They refused to listen to the prevailing data and instead chose to disrupt their industry. As a result, they ushered in another golden age of television.

It started with *The Sopranos*, which all the other major networks had turned down. It's easy to look back on *The Sopranos* as almost inevitable, as if it were always meant to be. But as the late historian David McCullough was fond of pointing out, history didn't have to turn out the way it did. Things could have gone in a much different direction.

This was the case in the early 2000s when HBO saw *The Sopranos* as a new and edgy type of series. They wanted creator David Chase on board to attract not only more viewers but more shows of this type. The network spent nearly $3 million on the pilot alone. But after showing the pilot to focus groups who gave it a big thumbs down, HBO leader Jeff Bewkes decided to push past this "bad data" and forge ahead. He knew in his gut that audiences would learn to love these unsympathetic characters, even if they weren't quite ready for it.

The Sopranos became a huge hit, earning 112 Emmy nominations over six seasons. Today, critics and viewers agree that this Shakespearean tragedy about a modern American crime family is one of the greatest TV series of all time.

With this success, HBO approached writer Alan Ball, who had just won an Oscar for the film *American Beauty*, about an idea for a show set in a funeral parlor. They gave him one rule: "Smash some china." They wanted him to break all the rules and weren't concerned with him creating characters who were likable, as long as they were interesting. The resulting series was *Six Feet Under*.

Word began to get out to Hollywood creatives that they could push the boundaries at HBO. Viewers almost hated themselves for loving these HBO characters, and their reaction was always strongest when the storylines didn't go the way they wanted. The next HBO show was *The Wire*, a crime drama set in Baltimore. It was also a critical success and showed how far the network would let writers push the limits.

HBO kept its word to creatives, and its shows received great reviews and word of mouth. Jeff Bewkes felt that success was better than cash. More is not better—better is better. Their awards started piling up in 2002, and HBO's name soon became synonymous with quality. It's a reputation that still stands today.

Let's look at another example from an entirely different industry. Southwest Airlines, which happens to be one of my favorite airlines, has outperformed the S&P 500 year after year. Sometimes, they are the only profitable airline stock. You could make a pretty good argument that they're exceptional at what they do. The way Southwest accomplishes this is by staying true to its culture and values and not operating just on financial data.

Years ago, when the legendary Herb Kelleher was CEO, their analysts went to him and said, "You know, all the other airlines are charging money for customers to check their luggage, but we're offering two bags for free. You're leaving $300 million on the table. Why would you do that?"

As the story goes, Herb sat there for a while. Then he famously said, "If I charge for luggage, more people are going to put their items in the overhead bins. This means my flight attendants, who are smiling at customers and taking care of their needs, will become baggage handlers, which they are on other airlines. The customers and flight attendants will have a worse experience, and it will take longer for us to board our planes and turn them around, which will decrease our profitability."

What a great example of going against the data and looking at the bigger picture of profitability, employee experience, and customer satisfaction. In an age when most airlines struggle to stay profitable,

Southwest led the pack in customer satisfaction. That is, until December 2022, when their aging infrastructure caused a total cancellation of flights and a meltdown of trust. If Herb were still around, that never would have happened.

Can Data Make Us Better Artists?

Let me close this chapter by making a few observations about data and algorithms, and their value in helping us become better Business Artists.

When I talk to technologists, particularly those focused on human and user design, they will tell me that really good technology is invisible. One of the reasons we don't think about the implications of technology is that it's so integrated into our lives that we don't even realize it's there.

If you watched Netflix and it didn't have recommendations or was missing the *Continue Watching* feature when an episode ended, you'd have noticed it and been annoyed. You'd be frustrated if you showed up to work and had to re-log in to all the apps and websites you use. Technology has made it ridiculously easy to continue with the same processes day after day or month after month. We don't think twice about jumping right back into the repetitive workflow with no friction.

But does all this actually help us be better employees, salespeople, and leaders? We're so used to the presence of technology that we don't even question whether it's helping us be better humans.

Case in point: consider David Cope's musical algorithm, Experiments in Music Intelligence (EMI). Cope is a Professor of Musicology at the University of California, Santa Cruz. His EMI program was composed so well that when its Bach-style pieces were heard by music lovers, they couldn't differentiate between EMI's pieces and authentic Bach![1]

That's just one example. Technology, data, and algorithms are increasing in speed and power on a nearly daily basis. But it's not just technology. *We're* also speeding up, and we expect everything to be increasingly more efficient, faster, and better.

So where does that leave us? For all the convenience of tech and automation, it's actually making us *less* human. While speed and convenience give us a short-term boost, over the long term, they are subject to the law of diminishing returns.

Test this theory the next time you visit Starbucks. When you order a venti coffee at 6:00 a.m. and take that first sip, it's nice. You get that immediate satisfaction of caffeine coursing through your veins. You drink half of it, but it's a little less satisfying with each sip. By the end, you are just drinking it because it's there. It turns out that even though it was convenient, in the end, it was really nothing special.

The next time you go back, try this. Don't give the barista a specific order. Instead, tell them what you're in the mood for. They will give you recommendations based on your mood. Then, they prepare a custom drink order for you that you savor down to the last drop. Tomorrow, you'll know a bit more about what you want, and you'll value the barista's knowledge and the artistry required to give you a customized drink.

If you follow this line of thinking, you'll start to appreciate it in the way you work with different vendors. When you value customization, individuality, and human connection instead of just convenience and speed, it will lead to more fulfilling experiences. Who knew that a single cup of coffee could have such a profound effect on your work?

Such is the power of the Business Artist approach. When you try new things instead of assuming that faster and more convenient is better, it will change your experience.

I hope the previous few chapters haven't been a *downer*. But I believe in being honest about what I see in the world of business, particularly as it applies to sales and creativity. There is much at stake— everything, in fact.

In the next chapter, I'll do my best to articulate what lies ahead over the next few decades and help us understand how to take advantage of this incredible moment in human history.

5

IF THESE SHADOWS REMAIN

In Charles Dickens' classic story, *A Christmas Carol*, the miserly Scrooge is haunted by three ghosts. He is disturbed by what each of them shows him.

The Ghost of Christmas Past haunts Scrooge, reminding him of his mistakes that caused unnecessary grief and pain. The Ghost of Christmas Present haunts Scrooge by showing him a different perspective on what is happening now. And the Ghost of Christmas Yet to Come haunts him with a vision of what will happen if the present course of action continues unaltered.

During Scrooge's visit with the Ghost of Christmas Yet to Come, the ghost reveals the grave of Tiny Tim and declares, "If these shadows remain unaltered by the future, the child will die."

Although *A Christmas Carol* is fiction, it has stayed embedded in popular culture because it shows us a basic human truth: Our actions today have profound consequences for tomorrow.

After reading the last few chapters, you may feel a bit like Scrooge after he visits with the three ghosts. It all seems like bad news leading to an inevitable future where we become unwilling subjects of the computers that will conquer us. As we stand before these apparitions, haunted by what we've seen, we wonder, *Is there anything we can do to alter the outcome?*

My goal in diving into the three problems we've addressed in detail in Part 1—Imitation, Perception, and Automation—isn't to make things look hopeless. Instead, my goal is to be honest about where things stand. If we don't have an accurate reading of where we are now, how can we possibly navigate what's sure to be turbulent waters ahead?

I don't want to sound melodramatic, but I can't escape the truth. If these shadows remain unchanged, something will die. That *something* is the opportunity for Business Artists like you and me to have a lasting impact not only on our own businesses but on the world as well.

Yes, I do mean "the world." Everything affects everything else. It used to sound grandiose to cling to the idea of "changing the world," but in an age where we're all hyper-connected, it no longer sounds far-fetched.

Change is inevitable. As much as we don't want to admit it, change always means death. For something new to arise, something has to die and make way for it. The old ways die, and from those ashes rise new perspectives, methods, and ideas.

It's up to us to determine what will rise from those ashes. Will it be a wonderful new world where Business Artists thrive? Or will it be a dark reality where we've abdicated our creative potential to codes and algorithms?

We all hope for the first option. But for that to happen, we need to understand where we're headed if things remain unchanged. Like Ebenezer Scrooge, we must first glimpse a terrifying vision of the future if we want to begin changing it.

In this chapter, I want to take you on a tour of where I see business and culture heading over the next decade or two. We'll focus on several topics, from innovation, creative thinking, and the arts to the metaverse, salespeople, human connection, and lots of areas in between.

It feels a little intimidating to put down my thoughts here. Who knows in five or ten years if they will be right? But just as the movie *Back to the Future Part II* got some things both right and wrong about life in the year 2015, I imagine I'll have a balance of both as well. I'll give it my best shot anyway. I'm thankful to have you come along as my companion as we tour the future together.

General Business Trends

Let's begin with a couple of trends, one on the consumer side and the other on the corporate side.

It's obvious we will continue to see more personalization of goods and services, in addition to targeted marketing and customized recommendations. These have been around for years with the advent of technology to create them. Netflix, Amazon, and every social media platform give you recommendations based on points of data they have about you.

In generations past, if you wanted to know what music to listen to, what TV shows to watch, what to wear, who to date, or where to travel, you listened to your friends or family. Although word of mouth is still the best marketing vehicle, we increasingly rely on tech to make our decisions for us.

It's easy to decry this and say, "The robots are taking over the world!" But on the other hand, it's pretty convenient when Amazon, Netflix, or Spotify recommend something we know we will love. If robots do take over the future, it won't be because we hated them and fought a war till death. It will be because we loved them and willfully surrendered.

As for how this trend of personalized recommendations will affect Business Artists, it will make it more difficult, in some ways, because fewer creators will take bold steps to challenge the status quo. When you interrupt people's relationships with the tech they use on a daily basis, you'll wind up with a fight on your hands.

From the standpoint of those creating these tools and technology, there will come a time when we recognize that we've created a monster. Then, we will stop being enamored with how personalization and recommendations serve us. The ever-increasing explosion of business productivity tools and data-driven insights will stop being helpful at some point. We will realize we can no longer think for ourselves, just like a person who uses a calculator for complex functions but soon finds themselves reaching for it to add 8+13.

In other words, we are continuing to delegate more and more decision-making to our technology. If tech only gives us what we want, we have strangled curiosity and creativity to the point where they can no longer breathe.

We should want to use the tools but not be used *by* them. Over time, we will find that we have less and less free will because we have succumbed to data-fueled, passive decision-making that gives us a sense of control. But in fact, we are the ones being controlled.

Looking at the broader business world, we will continue to see the dominance of a few companies that control more and more aspects of our lives. And with that trend comes its by-product, which is the consolidation of power into the hands of a few. That's not a new trend, of course. Humans have been trying to consolidate power ever since the days of smaller tribes joining together to form larger ones in order to dominate their regions. But the way that tech companies are dominating our lives is new.

The biggest danger in so few individuals having so much control is that when a big system fails, it fails hard. There are drastic consequences that impact us in profound ways.

Do you remember a few years ago when Google services were offline for a day or two? It practically shut down the internet because we all rely on Google so much. That's just the tip of the iceberg of how much power and influence we have given a few companies.

That's a broad look at where business might be headed. Let's turn our attention to the world of sales.

The World of Sales

Here's a question to ponder: Is there even going to be a need for salespeople in the year 2030?

Looking to the future, we may need to consider that salespeople will play a different role in business since there are more automation tools and demand generation created by computers. In the past, I made sales because I called a lot of people. The result was directly tied to my input.

But that inside sales approach is going away. As a result, the job of a salesperson will go one of two ways.

The first possibility is that salespeople will transition to a role that requires higher brain function. All other aspects will be driven by AI-led generation and other outreach, including proposals, quote requests, and initial calls with customers. Gartner, a research and consulting company, made the following prediction: "By 2025, 30 percent of outbound marketing messages from large organizations will be synthetically generated, up from less than 2 percent in 2022."[2]

As a result, customers will go to your website to buy or demo your product for themselves. They won't need to talk to you for that part.

There will be fewer salespeople, but those who remain will be skilled in other ways where they haven't needed to be in the past. This will be especially important with high-ticket items or enterprise sales, where consumers will probably still want human connection, guidance, and service.

In addition, the most successful salespeople in the future will be the ones with high critical thinking skills and emotional intelligence. F. Scott Fitzgerald described intelligence as the ability to hold two opposing thoughts in your head at the same time. This is an extremely important skill when you are in the middle of a sales conversation. You must hold your own thought and your customer's opposing thought together at the same time.

The other possibility is the complete opposite, where data controls all the sales functions, and salespeople are just doing what the computer tells them to do. They have to add a bit of their own intelligence, but that scenario will diminish over time as most sales functions are taken over by technology.

Customers are becoming more empowered to perform much of the buying process on their own. The process might involve empowering customers and destroying the role of salespeople at the same time. It's easy to decry this sort of development, but hasn't this always been the case in the world of business?

The world of auto sales has been moving in this direction for many years. When was the last time you bought a new or used car without knowing the Kelly Blue Book price? It's probably been a while. Customers know what the dealer makes on sales, so they feel empowered to haggle. Therefore, the role of the auto salesperson is not to give information but to provide such a personalized experience that customers enjoy the process of buying.

Not a bad model to follow for a salesperson in any industry.

The Metaverse

One of the more controversial trends is the metaverse. We all know it's here to stay in some form, but in what way? Ultimately, I imagine the metaverse will usher in a wave of disinterest in real life. If you can do anything and everything in the 'verse, why spend time in the real world? At least, that will be the thinking of some people. It sounds fringe now but will become more mainstream as there are more applications for the metaverse to real-world problems.

At first, the metaverse will become a place for new forms of creativity and expression. And what a fantastic opportunity for Business Artists! We will be able to discover new ways of working, collaborating, and engaging with clients and customers when the audience reaches a critical mass.

But as the metaverse matures and becomes normalized, more people will find ways to create and express that they hadn't before— almost as if they can become someone totally different than they are in "real life." To take it a step further, we will start erasing the boundaries between "real life" and the metaverse. As life in the metaverse matures, we will develop laws and regulations to govern how we operate, just as we do in the physical world.

We've seen a bit of this since there have already been reports of assault and other inappropriate behavior there. Like all new technology, it brings out the best and the worst in people.

I'm not afraid to say that I'm bullish on the metaverse. It has the potential to impact all aspects of culture. Right now, it's a *blue ocean* where there are no specific rules or precedents on how we're supposed to interact and operate, but that may change over time.

The Importance of Divergent Thinking

One of my favorite questions to ask executive audiences is, "What would have to be true?" When you are trying to imagine a different future, it's a great question to help you consider what needs to change in your current situation to fulfill your vision. "What would have to be true?" is an open-ended question that opens up possibilities.

What we usually say is, "No, that won't work. Let me tell you why." We are so used to assuming we can't change the future that we give up before we even start. Hence, the importance of divergent thinking, which literally helps us diverge from our current pathway.

I also love having executives draw out the ecosystem of how the world works, or at the very least, how their part of their business works today. I ask them to consider questions like these:

- Where does the money come from?

- Where do the customers come from?

- Where does talent come from?

- What regulatory rules are in place today?

- What might change in the future?

Then I have them start to ruminate on which of those rules we have created and which are laws of nature that cannot be broken. I also have them consider which rules we could change if we wanted. This exercise is powerful because it shows that most of the processes governing our behavior are not immutable laws of nature. Rather, they are *rules* that can be broken.

This is how disruptive thinking occurs. It's what Amazon does when it enters new markets. They look at how it's done today and then imagine how they could do it differently using their principles and techniques. How would Amazon do groceries, spaceflight, a smart home, and dozens of other categories of products or services?

The latest area Amazon is going into is healthcare, first with a pharmacy, and then with the acquisition of ONE Medical Group. They continue to enter new markets that have been dictated too long by one set of rules. Then, they change those rules.

If we stop thinking critically, we will stop challenging our preconceived notions. Eventually, we will lose the ability to innovate as we watch automation and computer intelligence supplant human thinking.

Why We Need Artists

This loss of critical thinking and a commitment to the status quo only highlights the need for truly artistic businesspeople. If you look honestly at the progress of AI and related technologies, it's pretty obvious that some jobs will be replaced by machines.

But it goes beyond that. As time goes on, it's not just simple or repetitive tasks that AI will take over. It will also perform increasingly creative work. Ultimately, human creativity will start to dwindle and feel like a lost art altogether.

Today, we have plenty of examples of lost human artistic capabilities. For example, humans used to use flowers and other organic materials to create fabric dyes. Today, there are countless other arts in danger of extinction, including stained glass making, acoustic musical instrument making, heritage masonry, natural perfume making, and the list goes on.

For example, Michael Pollard is the author of several food-themed books, including *The Omnivore's Dilemma* and *In Defense of Food*, which was also turned into a PBS documentary following his work with a group of kids who grew up in poor Brooklyn. They primarily eat processed food, like most Americans. The kids are brought into a program where they learn where their food comes from and how to grow it themselves. The kids are astonished because they had no idea where their food came from and that anyone could grow it on their own.

Our loss of creative, intellectual, and critical thinking skills isn't just about business. It also impacts every facet of life and trickles down to younger generations.

One of the ways it impacts them, and every age group, is that it makes it harder to deal with uncertainty, setbacks, and failure. When you've had the help of technology your whole life, what happens when the system fails or gets disrupted? A hundred years ago, our ancestors had a whole set of skills that have mostly been lost today.

Even so, there is cause for hope! These movements present excellent opportunities for Business Artists. Machines can't replace human empathy and intuition. These are the types of jobs that can't be quickly automated.

As a result, there will be a higher demand for creative thinkers. Companies will need to be able to not just retain their best talent but recruit them as well. AI will not replace your whole sales workforce. It will augment and automate some of the functions, but the best businesspeople who can connect on a human level will always be in demand.

The Future of Work

We're only beginning to see the changes that will take place in the way we think about work. The COVID-19 pandemic did not cause these shifts—they only accelerated trends already in progress. One of the biggest changes we're seeing in the corporate world is the loss of traditional nine-to-five jobs. For example, in the startup world, people are offering their services as fractional C-suite leaders—CFO, CEO, CRO, and more.

When people have the technology that gives them the ability to accomplish more, faster, they have more choices and more free time. They can use that time to do more creative tasks or perhaps just say, "I'm going to go home now because the job is done for me."

The result will be two classes of workers. The first will be those who want to be Business Artists. They want to spend their extra time innovating and creating. It's what they do. It's their purpose. It's what drives them.

The other group will be the equivalent of what I would call white-collar factory workers. They clock in, clock out, and perform a job that is mostly automated. They take in a little information or a pre-programmed set of instructions, do the work, and move on.

Over time, you will be able to choose which direction you want to go (or the choice will be made for you). We might even change the way we think about highly skilled workers. What seems like a highly skilled ability today may be a simple automated task tomorrow.

Since this chapter is titled "If These Shadows Remain," let's take a quick look at the shadow side of the future of work.

One of the aspects of a doomsday scenario might be the decline of the modern company in the sense that we know it. You might have fewer full-time employees but more and more contractors doing jobs. They will probably have more decisions that humans used to make become automated decisions. Companies might become larger while actually having fewer employees due to the technology available to them. But is this necessarily a bad thing?

Over the last decade, we have seen a trend of more and more people building side hustles. One of the most attractive elements of a side hustle is that you can set your own hours and make all the decisions. You're no longer controlled by *the man*.

People no longer get the fulfillment they once did from traditional jobs. Who really wants to stand in an assembly line for eight hours a day? How does that bring you any meaning aside from getting a paycheck?

If we don't find ways to inject more meaning into work, we will continue to have a more stagnant and disengaged workforce. The last few years of the pandemic have shown us that many people are willing to forgo or reduce their paychecks to have more balance in their lives. Money is no longer the sole driving force behind many people's decisions on how and where to work.

Where is Automation Headed?

Have you ever stood in the grocery store line trying to decide whether to go to the self-checkout line or the regular register with a clerk? On one hand, you want the convenience of self-checkout, but you also realize there's value in the human connection.

The same is true for customers. As time goes on, customers will be doing more of the buying on their own, even for complex buying processes. Sellers will need to change the way they operate and focus less on automated and more on solid relationships.

For customers who need a human touch, great salespeople will be invaluable. They will find new artistic and creative ways to serve the customers, even when it involves a measure of automation. Perhaps it will be an interesting blend of high-tech and high-touch.

There's no reason to have a totally negative view of automation. It could free us up to focus more on creativity and innovation. When you have more free time, you can spend it doing higher-value work.

At the same time, we have to be honest and admit that when people have more free time, it's not as if they're always going to go pounding the pavement and thinking creatively about how they can do their jobs better. It's like the scenario when you go on vacation for two weeks and start to get bored after three days. Highly driven people are always looking for ways to be better and don't necessarily want to have vast amounts of free time and leisure.

We might also see *too much* automation. This scenario is not hard to imagine. Highly skilled laborers could be lost in sales and relationship management. Everything could start to move toward personal marketing and demand generation. In this situation, you don't care about who is calling who. You just want to make sure the job gets done.

It's hard to imagine, though, that we will ever move into a time when we don't value human connection. Once the pandemic started to subside, there was a huge renewed interest in live events, concerts, conferences, and all kinds of other ways for people to connect in person.

If robots eventually take over the world, at least we will be together in person to witness our final destruction! This leads us to the next section.

The Search for Connection and Purpose

As humans, we are wired to find meaning in the context of relationships. The friends, colleagues, clients, and customers who are part of our work life all contribute to our sense of belonging to the collective whole.

But as more work is automated, displaced workers will lose some of that sense of connection and purpose. We are at our best when we are challenged in ways that force us to grow. Many work situations will feel like the opposite as people's jobs transition into processes that don't give them the opportunity to improvise or work from their strengths.

As a person who has been in sales for a long time, I can verify that when salespeople are disconnected and don't find purpose in their work, they don't perform at their best. I have a simple way to help salespeople define their purpose. I ask, "If you could make more money and do less work elsewhere, why are you still here?" If they don't have a quick and meaningful response, you may have a seller who doesn't find much purpose in their job, or at least not with your company.

The more impersonal the company, the lower the switching costs are for sellers, and the easier it is for employees to quit. This is especially true for Business Artists who thrive on creativity and human connection. They can be the first to leave if their style of work is not permissible. However, they can also be the most loyal if they can see their creative ideas come to life over and over again. This is true of every industry and every type of work. No matter what type of work you do, you want to feel connected and have a higher sense of belonging.

One of the most important areas of human connection is the rise of diversity, equity, and inclusion training in the corporate world. While the goals of this kind of training are admirable, the training itself tends to be very procedural. For example, "If this micro-aggression happens, do this or this."

The training typically doesn't help people to think enough with intuition, which is essential for these topics. When learning the skills, we need interaction. We need to debate. We need reflection. Soft skills cannot be dumped into an employee's brain the same way an Amazon driver dumps a package on your front porch.

We avoid going deep with this kind of training because it's hard and makes us uncomfortable. As a culture, we are getting less and less able to deal with being uncomfortable. We've dealt with a high degree of uncertainty and cultural upheaval over the last few years. It's clear that mental health challenges are rising not just in young people but at every age. These challenges will not improve unless we take action to deal with him.

What Now?

As I mentioned near the beginning of this chapter, change is inevitable, and change always means death. By definition, change means something has died, and something new has risen from those ashes.

After reading this chapter, I hope you will not be discouraged, but rather motivated to act. We can look at the changes happening in the world, and we can bury our heads in the sand. But I hope we will not just accept what is happening and, instead, choose to prepare and find ways to be Business Artists who offer skills and perspectives that technology could never replace.

Will our creativity and artistry go the way of the dodo bird, relegated to the ashes of history? Or will we take our cue from the legendary Phoenix, rising to glory from the ashes of what once was?

Yes, change is hard and frightening. But over the past century, humankind has managed to do the impossible and rein in famine, plague, and (most of the time) war. Today, more people die from obesity than from starvation—more people die from old age than from infectious diseases—and more people die from suicide than are killed in wars. We have become complacent, but that complacency is no longer serving as well.

Now that we have spent a few chapters looking at some possible scenarios for the future in Part 2, we will consider some pathways we can take as Business Artists. I couldn't be more excited about the opportunities before us!

PART 2

MELODY

THE PATHWAY
OF THE BUSINESS ARTIST

6

THE ONLY WAY FORWARD

The quiet town of Cortez sits in the southwestern corner of Colorado. With a population of less than 10,000, Cortez is less famous and not as flashy as Denver, Aspen, or Telluride.

But if you ever visit Cortez, it's worth your time to drive south on Highway 491, then west on Highway 160. After a short jaunt off the highway, you will arrive at one of the most fascinating tourist attractions in the United States.

The Four Corners Monument is the only place in the United States where four states (Colorado, Utah, Arizona, and New Mexico) converge into a single point. If you sit in the middle of the giant seal that marks the spot, with your legs spread out and leaning back on your hands, you can literally be in four places at once.

This geographical marker is a good metaphor for this moment in time. We stand at a great convergence point where technology, trade, and world events have forced us to decide the pathway we will take. People throughout history have always faced decisions, but this is different. The next decade represents a critical point for humanity where we must decide how we will relate to technology and what our pathway forward will be as humans.

In Part 1, we looked at three problems facing business leaders today. I gave a fairly bleak picture, followed by a chapter describing what the future could look like.

Here in Part 2, I want to give you a more hopeful vision of what our pathway forward can look like. In Part 1, I used the theme of *dissonance* to describe the chaotic forces surrounding us, just like dissonant musical notes cause you to cringe just a bit. In this part of the book, I'll transition to the theme of *melody* to describe our way forward.

What is a melody, exactly? It's a blend of rhythm, voice, pitch, and timing to create a musical journey through the song. The melody of a song should be unmistakable. When a song is recorded but not mixed properly by a sound engineer, the melody gets lost in the background vocals and instruments.

In the same way, we have to make sure that, as Business Artists, we do not get lost in the chaos of the modern world. That's why, in this chapter, I will begin with three visions for our collective future, naturally arguing for the pathway of the Business Artist. It is the only viable way forward if we want to retain our true humanity and creative potential.

Vision One: The Path of Techno-Humanism

You may not have heard the term *techno-humanism* before. Yuval Noah Harari talks about the concept in his book *Homo Deus: A Brief History of Tomorrow*. The term refers to the merger of humans with technology to keep pace with the power of algorithms. Instead of using technology or submitting to it, we *become* it.[3]

This is already happening. The United States Army is developing a device called an *attention helmet*. It would send electrical signals to specific parts of the brain to help soldiers concentrate better for extended periods. This would make specialized soldiers, such as snipers or drone operators, as dependable as algorithms.

The types of technological upgrades available will, of course, reflect our political and economic needs. Considering our current tensions with China and Russia, these will surely be in flux over the coming years. The attention helmet is currently getting funding because it has clear military applications.

We will continue to see some elements of humans merging with technology. In the last few years, wearable tech, such as Apple Watches or Fitbits, has become commonplace. But when it's taken to an extreme, techno-humanism robs the essence of our humanity. As we've already talked about, empathy and human connection are essential to the pathway of the Business Artist.

The more we submit to technology and merge with it, the more we will lose the essence of what it means to be human. But I admit that I'm conflicted about it. I love technology and am fascinated by how we can use all the resources around us, whether they are natural resources or ones that we have created.

In the effort to drive greater competitive differentiation and greater performance, why don't we focus on using technology to help us in our human tasks?

Elon Musk's company, NeuroLink, is a great example. Musk's point of view is that it's good to have the world's information at our fingertips. But the problem he's trying to solve is how to access it and speed up the process. He's created a company that plants chips into human brains, featuring a Bluetooth receiver that hangs on your ear.

When you want to perform a task like typing a text message or searching for something on the internet, you don't have to pull out your phone and ask. You just think it.

That type of technology is scary to some people, but there's some value to it. Consider all the time you spend typing on your computer or phone and how much time that technology could save! Think of the possibilities for disabled individuals as well.

However, the downside of technology that makes our lives so efficient is that it releases us from the burden of creative thinking.

Most new tech startups I see are trying to create ways to use data more effectively so that people have to think less. Time savings are easy to measure, so generative tools embedded in workflows get justified quickly. This isn't a book about artificial intelligence, but AI is absolutely part of the mix since we have quickly adopted it for all kinds of uses.

Technology can make us more efficient and effective. It can perform all kinds of analysis that we could not do otherwise. But even with these admittedly powerful advantages, we must ask ourselves: Do we really want to create a future where humans have to think less?

Creative thinking is one of the basic factors that make humans—well, *human*. While we are rushing headlong into a future where we are eager to merge with everything new, maybe we should slow down for a moment and think about the ramifications of merging too much.

Vision Two: The Path of Dataism

The second vision differs from the first, although they feel the same on the surface.

Both visions involve a future where we depend on technology more and more. Whereas *techno-humanism* represents a merging of humans and technology, *dataism* represents a future where we leave our hands in the fate of data. It's a bit more nihilistic, perhaps even dystopian, when taken to its logical conclusion.

Dataism basically says that we should step aside and let algorithms just do their thing. Everything that exists is either a data processing system or an algorithm. It doesn't matter if it's the position of the sun, someone's political stance, or your lover's broken heart. It's all just data.

In addition, dataism does not see humanity as a fundamental, unique concept in the universe. It sees humans as computers that process data. We take in information and use that data to make decisions. Even something simple like shopping for groceries depends on your hunger, the weather, the time, your budget, the locations of stores in your area, or other factors. It's all data that factors into your eventual actions.

According to this perspective, history is just a process where we manufacture ever-improving data processing systems. Consequently, it's our duty as humans to build more efficient algorithms to process all this data. This viewpoint falls short for several reasons. For one thing, data is not enough to help you make good decisions. You can have the most detailed data in the world yet still come up short. We see this all the time in the world of sports.

Take football, for example. If someone can run a fast forty-yard dash, he must be able to be a great NFL running back, correct? Metrics like this are one of the ways that teams and scouts used to recruit players and winnow the field. Metrics have value, but that value has limits.

When you start to get into more highly-skilled positions such as a wide receiver or quarterback, football becomes an art. People in those positions don't have to be the fastest or strongest, but they do have to make the best decisions. The decision-making process of a winning quarterback can't be predicted or created by any NFL metrics, no matter how granular you get.

Hockey great Wayne Gretzky shared a wonderful insight on the Apple TV documentary *In Search of Greatness*: "It's making something important because we can measure it. It's not measuring it because it's important. ..."[4] You can measure lots of skills and include endless amounts of data to help you make decisions. But it's impossible to quantify the thinking process of world-class athletes like Wayne Gretzky, Tom Brady, or Albert Pujols.

The team with the best data doesn't always win. Data tells an incomplete picture that cannot account for unpredictable factors and the human drive that make sports so compelling in the first place.

Another problem with relying on data too heavily is that it's controlled by people who are *not* computers. Ultimately, human beings like you and me control every aspect of data, such as the information that's deemed important, how it's gathered and processed, and who gets to have access.

Anyone who's ever taken a basic statistics course knows that data can be interpreted many different ways. Numbers don't mean anything unless they are put into context by someone. You should only trust the meaning of data if you trust the people who are collecting, interpreting, and communicating it.

For example, did you know that the *New York Times* Best Sellers list is not actually a list of the books that sold the most copies? People in the publishing world have known for years that it's an editorial list.

Although the people who compile that list take certain sales data into account, it's actually a curated list that reflects the editors' picks for which books should be the most popular. (In all fairness, there can never be such a thing as a true bestseller list for books because it's impossible to account for all sales channels. For example, Amazon is a huge retailer, but they do not make their sales data public.)

Given all these factors, perhaps we should not leave our fate in the hands of data since it's ultimately humans who control it. If history has taught us anything, it is that humans, when left to their own devices, will do almost anything to protect themselves, including manipulating or withholding information. This is why totalitarian regimes are so terrible, and why checks and balances in any system are crucial.

Vision Three: The Path of the Business Artist

Given everything we've talked about in this book so far, and in light of technology that is improving every day, why should we choose the path of the Business Artist? How is it fundamentally different than techno-humanism or dataism?

The heart of the issue is the place we give technology in our lives. Is technology a passenger on the bus, or is it *driving* the bus?

If we relinquish our fate to technology, we have lost our way. We must rediscover what it means to be human. This leads to a fascinating question. Since artificial intelligence and technology are getting so good at mimicking human thinking, what is the role that humans play in the destiny of planet Earth if technology can do everything we can, but faster and better?

The point of life is not to do everything faster and better. The point of life is to experience it, to relate with other humans on the same journey, to take in the beauty of the universe, and in turn create our own beauty.

If your main goal is to make life more efficient, you have missed the very purpose of life itself.

When Theodore Roosevelt was president, he established the National Park system. He grew up in a period of rapid technological progress in American culture. Roosevelt had the foresight to use the federal government's power to protect areas where industry could not encroach. He believed the natural world was a gift to enjoy, not just a source of raw materials for industry. There were sections of land worth preserving because they added value and beauty to the human experience.

In the same way, the Business Artist says, "There is a human experience worth preserving at any cost, even if it means less efficiency or progress." If we let data and technology take over every aspect of our lives, there will be no experience left to have. The dystopian visions of the future in movies like *Blade Runner* or *The Matrix* don't seem so fictional when you consider the lighting pace of technological progress. This is why we need to protect what is essential about the human experience.

It will require boldness and courage. In the rest of this chapter, we'll focus on a few ways we must be courageous as we forge ahead.

The Courage to Empathize

When most salespeople consider what skills are essential to their profession, empathy probably does not make the top of the list. But I disagree with that point of view. Every successful salesperson I've ever met has a lot of empathy and can relate well with others.

If you're in sales, you not only need to be able to make the right phone calls and say the right words. You also must have an implicit, empathetic knowledge of who you're talking to. You need to be able to use all the resources in your natural environment, what we would call *technology*, to relate to that person.

Your goal is to move their business forward through a sale or a conversation that might lead to a sale. When you enter a conversation, you must figure out what that person is saying, doing, thinking, and feeling. Then, you must pivot the conversation to where you would like it to go, all with the intention of serving your client or customer well. This is the essence of effective communication.

Empathetic selling has been the subject of many books and much research. It's hard to do well if you have grown up in a data-driven world. If you live in a world tailored to your preferences, it feels like a lot of effort to focus on what someone else wants or needs.

You go home, and there is a Netflix recommendation about what you should watch. You visit a new place, and the GPS tells you the most convenient way to get there. A world of personalization and convenience means you explore less. As a salesperson, it's therefore harder to put yourself in someone else's shoes because technology is always putting itself in *your* shoes to make your life easier.

Every salesperson would benefit from going to a new city, renting an Airbnb, and then not using Google Maps to get around. There's a lot of value in going somewhere you've never been, then saying to yourself, "I'm going to find my way back. I don't know this city, but I'm smart and intuitive enough to figure it out."

You end up going in different directions and heading down dead ends as you find your way. You're not following a script. Instead, you're discovering new places and using creative thinking to explore the world. You're putting yourself in other people's shoes and experiencing what it's like to live there. That's the essence of empathy.

The Courage to Create

As humans, we are wired to consume. We wake up thinking about what we will wear, eat, watch on streaming, or buy. Even though creativity is a natural human impulse, we are so distracted and oriented toward consumption that creativity takes intentional effort.

Creation requires courage. Consumption does not.

The more we rely on technology to give us what we want, the more it is a struggle to create. This is not only true in life. It's true of the sales process as well. If you always have a playbook or process to guide you on how to talk to a CFO or a COO, then you haven't learned how to do this on your own.

While it may be easier to always have a guide or proven pathway, it also takes away the joy of exploration. It's no fun having technology do all the work for you. For example, it might be convenient to have every book in the world available for instant download, but then we've lost something important by not having to visit a local library or bookstore. When technology only serves you what you have consumed in the past, there's no discovery.

Creation requires courage because it means we don't just rely on technology to do the work for us. We understand the value of getting our hands dirty and walking "among the stacks" of life.

The creative process must be intentional. The more we focus on consuming and making ourselves comfortable in life, the duller our creative senses become. It's not an automatic process. As much as we would like to believe that age and life experience will make us more creative, it's simply not true. You don't become more creative by getting older. You become more creative by making things, taking risks, dissecting other people's work, and paying attention.

The Courage to Experiment

As children, we loved to play and experiment. We're discovering where we fit into the big picture of life. Over time, we have a better understanding of our gifts and the unique ways we might be able to contribute to the world.

But once we gain knowledge in a particular career, we are less prone to experiment. We play by the rules, and most of us go to great lengths to avoid rocking the boat. As "responsible adults," we do what we once thought unthinkable. We settle for the status quo.

Theoretical physicist Richard Feynman was a good example of doing just the opposite. Although he won a Nobel Prize and was revered by people for his depth of knowledge, in his research, he also kept in mind what he called "open problems" or open questions. As he went through life, he would always ask, "Does this have anything to do with my open question?"

It's fun to take this perspective and find connections across domains that, on the surface, might not seem to be connected. He saw life as one giant experiment with questions still to be settled.

I encourage you to visit any contemporary or modern art museum. You don't have to like it all or agree with the experimentation, but you have to appreciate the attempt and bring that quality into your work. This goes beyond "thinking outside the box." We're talking about *thinking forward* and finding your creative style.

The very nature of being an artist is creating something that hasn't existed before. We all have influences, and nobody is truly "original." Everything is a riff on what's come before. But at its core, all art is experimentation because you're expressing yourself in a way the world has never seen in that exact way.

The "old masters" of painting typically focused on one style until they had taken it as far as their skills would let them. Change happened slowly. When change happens fast, people perceive it as "chaos" or "art expression."

This experimentation is what artists love to do. It takes courage to experiment and not constrain yourself to the pace the marketplace can handle. This is why many artists are considered "avant-garde" in their generation, but by the next generation, they're considered "old school."

The term "avant-garde" comes from the French and literally means *advance guard*, referring to the part of the army that goes forward ahead of the rest. I can't think of a better metaphor for Business Artists. We go forward and pave the way for others with empathy, creation, and experimentation.

In the next chapter, we will take this a step further as we explore the mind of a Business Artist.

7

THE ARTISTIC MIND

I'm a verbal thinker. I do my best thinking when I'm talking, unlike a visual thinker who processes information best by seeing. I remember things I read or hear aloud. I'm also a sponge for historical information and love to speak in metaphors, especially those that involve common historical knowledge.

Here's an example from years ago. I was wrapping up a strategic sales workshop for a large software client. Afterward, I approached the sponsor, also the head of sales. He had just delivered an ending keynote to the audience. I was hoping we might have dinner together to build a more personal relationship.

When I asked, he said, "Eh, I think I'm busy."

I replied, "Come on, don't be King John the II!"

He said what most people would say in that situation. "Who's King John the II?"

This is a great example of how to begin a story. The listener is asking you to share and giving you permission to engage them. You can take the feedback they give you as you're talking and choose to wrap up quickly or go even deeper if they seem interested.

Whenever I share my King John story with others, it goes something like this:

"Who is King John II, you ask? Well, if you'll allow me, the story of old King John II actually starts about thirty years prior. It begins with a boy born in Genoa, Italy. This kid, a smart and handy lad, gets into the family business with his father. They build ships and become quite good at it.

"One day, this bustling young man says, 'I don't just want to make ships, I want to sail them.' And where would a young man with sea-faring ambitions go in those days? To the largest shipping empire in the world at that time, of course: Portugal. So, this kid, who had become a man by then, headed west and found himself wanting more. He wanted to be an entrepreneur. He had a great idea, but it would need some funding. So where did he go? None other than your boy, John—King John, that is.

"Now, getting into the court of King John II was no easy task—just as hard as it is for someone like me to be getting direct access to you, one might say. But back to our story. This entrepreneurial dreamer went into the court of King John II, laid out his plans, and said, 'I just need a little money, what do you say?' And just like you, King John II said 'eh' without really considering that some decisions, no matter how small, will ripple through eternity.

"Now, this kid was crushed and devastated, but he pulled himself together and came back a second time. His heart was racing as he laid out his bold idea and asked for capital. But again, King John II said, 'Eh, not interested.' The boy nearly fell to the floor, his dreams crushed, but once again, he pulled himself together.

"This time, he went east to a smaller and less powerful region of the world called Castille. He went into the court of Isabella and Ferdinand and asked the Spanish crown for money and support. Of course, that year was 1492, that boy was Christopher Columbus, and King John is the reason nobody speaks Portuguese in the world."

"Now, can I take you out for dinner tonight or not?"

The first time I used that story, I had just read the section on Columbus from Howard Zinn's *The People's History of the United States* and subsequently watched some YouTube videos on Portuguese history, so I had been thinking about it quite a bit. My artistic mind was able to get into a flow state, pulling in recent information, translating it back into what was in front of me, and animating it in such a way that got the sales leader to decide to come out to dinner.

Even better, he had me share that story with several strangers we met that night. I added or subtracted certain pieces according to the conversation.

Now that we have spent several chapters establishing the problems we're facing in business today, and showing that the pathway of the Business Artist is the only way forward, I want you to think about a fundamental question. *What exactly does it mean to be an artist, anyway?*

This is a complicated question, but I want to simplify things by focusing on a few key qualities of the artistic mind. This chapter serves two purposes. First, it will help you assess the qualities you'd like to develop and celebrate the ones you already have. And second, it will help leaders understand their team members better and help them operate at their full potential as Business Artists.

Dozens of qualities can define an artist, but let's focus on four critical ones. Through my own research, and dialogue with lots of sales leaders and professional consultants, I'm more convinced than ever that this list rings true of all artists, especially the ones who are successful in business and sales.

1. Artists Have Active Minds

People who have creative minds find it difficult to shut off their curiosity. There is no "pause button," and if there were, they wouldn't want to use it anyway. This way of approaching life can be exhausting, but it's also the source of endless creative activities and inspiring conversations.

One of the best examples of a curious thinker I've ever seen is my former colleague Marta Zaragoza, who leads the Southern Europe and Latin America team for BTS. Marta has a reputation for always going a thousand miles per hour. She is intensely curious with clients and always tries to learn more.

One of Marta's team members, Miguel Sequeira, mentioned that anytime a client opportunity is paused after a couple of days, Marta quickly asks, "What can we do? What are the reasons? How are they viewing this and us?" Marta's approach is wonderful because it helps the team look for creative solutions.

The obsession with curiosity is the central driving force of the overactive mind. Many times over the years, I've told friends and colleagues that I'm a social theorist. I am obsessed with asking "why" as it relates to all aspects of human performance in social and business settings. Why will certain people speak first in a room? Why do certain people feel compelled to challenge the status quo when others passively accept it? Why won't this work, why does this work, why hasn't this worked?

"Why" is a powerful question. Sometimes, I even ask, "Why *do* we ask why?"

For example, in a sales or business meeting, sometimes I ask "why" simply to learn or probe for additional knowledge. Or I may ask "why" to validate or challenge an already-held opinion or hypothesis. Sometimes, I ask "why" to understand how someone feels or where they are coming from.

And those are just the *why* questions! The mind never stops being curious, whether we're talking about *why*, or even *what* and *how* questions. But is it ultimately a good thing to have a mind that never slows down? If not, when can an active, racing mind get in the way of someone's success? Can it produce negative consequences?

Perhaps. I know that I can come across as obsessed or intense at times. I've had close friends say, "Adam, why don't you just enjoy life instead of trying to figure it out all the time?"

I naturally reply, "You don't understand. Trying to figure out life is how I enjoy it."

I've learned that I need to force myself to slow down at times, or I can quickly spiral into a cave of curiosity that has no end. If you don't do this, you will burn out from the never-ending adrenaline rush of intense curiosity.

It's also vital to partner with someone whom you trust, someone who knows how your mind works. I have a great colleague and friend, Matt Archer. He's a co-founder with me at Meahana. Our minds are very different. Matt is masterful at execution and, in his own artistic way, knows how to let my mind roam and get lost a bit. Then, he will summarize, add his points, and move forward. He helps to pace my thought process so the output is targeted to whatever we are working on.

Constraints and Curiosity

When I don't have a partner, I set other constraints. Great artistic output comes from constraints. If you play a certain note on a piano, you are already constrained mathematically to any good options you have next. It sounds counterintuitive, but it's true. Art is best built in a constrained universe.

Another way I constrain myself to slow down and pace myself is by setting clear *milestones* for my brain. I have output goals and questions I will answer by a certain time, then dedicate a block of time on my calendar to get it done. I have to be realistic about how much time it takes to get into a state of creative flow.

Earlier, I mentioned Marta as a great example of curiosity. In addition, let me tell you about Fredrik Schuller, another global partner at BTS and the head of the Coach Practice.

Fredrik is one of the first people I call when I want to dream up new solutions for a client problem. I know he will ask me lots of questions I had not considered. Then the two of us mentally co-create a solution together. We'll laugh at how ridiculous most of the solutions are in terms of our ability to actually execute them.

Even so, we spend a lot of time asking, "Wouldn't it be cool, though?" We will eventually bring in other minds into the conversation to help slow us down, ground us in reality, and find something practical we can execute.

My client, Travis Jones, also loves to explore new possibilities and creative solutions to problems. Travis is a sales enablement leader at Autodesk. His mind is similar to Fredrik's in that once the objectives have been defined, he doesn't settle on what has been done before but rather on what we haven't tried that would be new and interesting.

Travis is the only person I know who brought an escape room concept to a sales kickoff where we were already doing competitive interactive simulations with actual customer involvement. Pulling it off took a lot of effort, but the result was an ambitious, exhausting, and rewarding experience for us and the sellers who attended.

These are the type of clients and colleagues I love to innovate with. They are filled with curiosity and creativity. Naturally, those qualities often lead to situations where you need to confront the status quo to build something better, which leads us to the next point.

2. Artists Challenge the Status Quo

Business Artists don't want to be order takers. Instead, they feel deeply for their customers and seek to identify the root cause of a customer issue. They don't do this just because it will lead to a potentially bigger deal, but because they care. Sometimes, they care too much, and this passion can backfire unexpectedly.

Artists in sales will not only challenge the status quo of their organization. They will also do this for their customers' organizations. They constantly ask *why* questions like *what if* or *why not?* They question what everyone else accepts at face value. *Why do we pitch this way? Why are we using this template? Why are we using this story?* The goal of the Business Artist is to redefine what is possible.

The idea of challenging the status quo and going up against preconceived notions may sound sexy and fun. But you have to be ready to defend it against forces of historical inertia, all while making compromises when necessary. This often means being able to highlight dissatisfaction as a first step to gaining buy-in on anything new.

If someone doesn't see a problem or experience it the same way you do, getting them to see a reason to change is pretty difficult.

I'll give an example. In my former role with BTS, we had a new offering. It was a sales assessment which was essentially a tool to evaluate candidates in the sales hiring process. This new offering created a powerful cloud-based simulation that would give candidates a realistic *day in the life* scenario to assess them and give them a flavor of the job they were applying for. It was better than anything available in the market at the time.

I was trying to position this to talent and recruitment buyers, who were some of my largest tech clients. They said, "Adam, this is cool. It's better than what we are doing today. The only thing is that the way we are doing it today seems to be working well enough for us right now. Unless that changes or becomes a problem, we don't see the need for us to look into anything new where we'd have to bring in a new platform and change our processes."

This taught me an important lesson. It's great to challenge the status quo, but you have to understand why someone would be interested in what you're selling. Is there enough dissatisfaction already that you can help them see in the current process? Does your concept take into consideration the existing investments and processes that need to be removed for anything new to gain interest?

If you don't understand where other people are coming from, how can you put yourself in their shoes and see the problem as they see it? Or even if it is a problem? That's a core component not only in sales but in human relationships as well.

Entrepreneurs and Solopreneurs

You may be thinking, *Adam, that's great, but I'm an entrepreneur* or, *I'm a solo business owner. How does this concept apply to me since I don't work in an organization or company?*

It applies *especially* to you because the very idea of starting a business means you are challenging the status quo. You are telling the market, "I'm not satisfied with the current products and services in my niche. I think I can do better or add value in some unique way." You're also challenging the status quo on a personal level because you are taking on risk and responsibility that was not there before.

If you run your own business, you must constantly be in the habit of asking three questions:

1. **Why change?** (Why should anyone do something different than what they have been doing? How can their lives be more efficient, profitable, or fun?)

2. **Why now?** (Why do your customers or clients need to act now, as opposed to a year or five years from now?)

3. **Why me?** (Why should they do business with you personally instead of going with a different company offering the same thing?)

We often think about the first question, but not necessarily the second and third ones. This is why you don't see everyone with a new idea jumping out the door to start their own company. It's one thing to have a great idea but quite another to bring it to market yourself.

3. Artists Think and Speak in Stories

In the previous chapter, I introduced the element of storytelling into the Business Artist framework. It's such a critical component of everything the Business Artist stands for that it's worth exploring in more detail here.

Facts will never move the human heart like storytelling can. Highly creative people, especially artists, know this. They weave stories into everything they do. Why? Because stories are the way we make sense of the world.

The oral tradition of storytelling in human history is powerful. This is the primary way our ancestors communicated information long before printing presses, typewriters, or computers existed.

The ancient Greeks were masters of storytelling. Today, you can pull down a copy of *The Iliad* or *The Odyssey* off your shelf or read them on your tablet, but that wasn't the case in the eighth century B.C. Those texts were created orally for performance, and then written down later. Both of those epic poems are long, which is a testament to the level of skill those creators and storytellers brought to the listening experience.

The same is true of the complex mythology they developed over time to explain natural phenomena. Our ancestors used stories to make sense of the world. If they didn't understand something like lighting or ocean waves, they made sense of it by creating characters such as Zeus or Poseidon.

Greeks weren't the only ancient people to use stories to develop culture and religion. For example, the Jewish and Christian traditions relied on oral tradition to pass on values and ideas through stories. In the Old Testament, the book of Psalms encourages the hearer to listen and tell stories: "My people, hear my teaching; listen to the words of my mouth. I will open my mouth with a parable; I will utter hidden things, things from of old—things we have heard and known, things our ancestors have told us" (Psalm 78:1-3, NIV).

In our modern world, we can access stories in every way you can imagine: books, movies, TV shows, comics, theater, live and recorded music, and much more. However, the best form of oral storytelling you'll see these days is stand-up comedy. If you begin to study stand-up, you'll pick up on various well-established comedy writing techniques. At the same time, you'll also see each comic following a different approach.

Sometimes, these are radically obvious differences and sometimes they are more subtle. But each one maximizes their unique personality and strengths on stage.

If you watch a Netflix special of any well-known comic, take some time to watch one of their earlier sets on YouTube. You'll hear many of the same jokes told in different styles and iterations. Sometimes, the joke is shorter or longer or involves someone from the audience. It's a fascinating study to see an artist constantly refining their work.

This line of thinking goes against current data and conformity-driven trends in business. My whole life, I've been told that brevity, word count, and the number of slides matter, as if there is a magic formula for a compelling sales presentation.

If it lacks a good story, it doesn't matter. On the other hand, if it has a story that draws the listener in, slides don't matter. A great story doesn't need to be communicated with slides to engage the audience. Think about your slide presentations as a connection of each story arc to the next. You'll learn the material faster and be able to animate it with authenticity.

How to Use Stories in Business

My peers and colleagues have told me again and again that storytelling is my primary strength. Even though I have a natural gift for it, I believe anyone can learn to improve their storytelling skills.

Here are seven tips that can dramatically improve your skills in this area:

1. **Start with a great hook.** The first episode of *Breaking Bad* began with an incredible opening sequence that grabbed your attention from the first second. A good story works the same way. Spend time crafting the first sentence or two of a story so it hooks your listener from the start.

2. **Use stories instead of case studies.** We've all heard a million case studies in business presentations, seminars, and workshops.

Can case studies be effective? Of course. But stories trump case studies every time because they lean on the story component (the most interesting part) rather than trying to analyze every detail of a story for deeper meaning.

3. **Communicate with the right motive.** We shouldn't use stories as a manipulative tactic just to make a sale. Instead, we are sharing them as a means to drive collaboration and connection. The goal is to invite someone to enter a specific part of our own human experience. This is why the best stories are not generic. They are personal to you.

4. **Make sure the story is relevant.** You must know your audience. More importantly, know what your audience doesn't know. What do they need to know about how your product or service or you can help them or improve their lives? Make sure to highlight that information in your stories.

5. **Include a proper amount of tension.** Imagine how much less effective Phil Collins's classic song "In the Air Tonight" would have been had he used drums in the first two-thirds of the song. Instead, he held off until the second chorus, knowing that the three-and-a-half minutes of tension would pay off in one of the most memorable drum fills in pop music. This is how stories should work as they build and release tension.

6. **Make your stories emotionally engaging.** This is where you need to use language and gestures to draw out the listener's experience. Do they need to feel joy? Pleasure? Distress? Delight? Sadness? Anxiety? Surprise? Fear? Play on those emotions to pull them into your story's world.

7. **Include a clear takeaway.** This is the reason you are sharing the story in the first place. You can state this up front and then again at the end of a story. For example, "I recently worked with another client who struggled with buyers not consuming their software post-sale. Would it be okay if I share a quick story of the work we did together that led to increased customer adoption?"

You may not feel like the world's greatest storyteller. But I guarantee that the more you practice, and the more you put yourself in situations where you can share stories with others, the better you'll get. Telling great stories is one of the most important skills any Business Artist can build.

4. Artists Need Space to Think and Create

People in the world of ancient Greece used two different words for the idea of time: *chronos* and *kairos*.[5] You probably recognize the word *chronos* as the root for the English words "chronological" and "chronicle." It refers to measured, ticking, and quantitative time. *Chronos* is the forward-propelling time that we measure with clocks, watches, and even the evolutionary phases of the moon. But time does not end there.

The second ancient Greek word for time, *kairos*, is lesser known but no less important. Kairos is what many philosophers and mystics refer to as "deep time." It's the time we're talking about when the world seems to stop entirely. It can be measured in deep exhales, a shared laugh, or a colorful sunset. *Kairos* is qualitative time where you can move forward in the present, untethered by any moving clock or calendar.

Franciscan Friar and author Richard Rohr refers to *kairos* as those moments in life that take your breath away.

Oh, my gosh. This is it. I get it.

This is as perfect as it can be.

It doesn't get any better than this.

We all know those moments, don't we? They may be few and far between, but sometimes a *kairos* moment can feed your soul for months. There is an element of serendipity, a feeling of seizing an opportunity, in those precious moments where time stands still and everything feels possible.

When you find yourself in *kairos* time, you completely lose track of *chronos* time. A state of flow is activated, and it cannot be measured.

It can only be experienced. This is why nostalgia is so powerful. Have you ever heard a song that instantly transported you back to a certain time and place? That's the power of *kairos* time.

All time is not created equal. When an artistic person is in their self-discovery or self-learning process, ten hours can feel like a hundred. They will be exhausted, as if they have been learning a new language. The creative process is not like walking or breathing, which you do in an unconsciously competent state. They don't require as much energy as when you are learning something for the first time.

When you are in *kairos* time, you are consciously incompetent. You're in learning mode because you're aware of what you don't know.

My goal with this book is to provide you with a *kairos* moment—one where time slows down and you are engaging your creative sensibilities. I hope the ideas here have helped you get into a flow state. What mental journeys, past or future memories, have you visited while reading?

Steven Pressfield, the author of *The War of Art*, writes, "Most of us have two lives. The life we live, and the unlived life within us. Between the two stands Resistance."[6] I love this quote because it translates to every successful Business Artist, especially if they work in a company that is on the nonlinear path from passion to process. In this type of culture, the creative energy that was once celebrated is now seen as a distraction to the mission.

You would be hard-pressed to find leaders in a company who would argue against more creativity and artistry. Most people understand the value of creative thinking. The problem comes when you have to allocate real time, money, and resources to help people be more creative.

Creativity cannot be relegated to a thirty-minute block between Zoom calls. People need space to think, learn, and refine products and projects. Sellers, in particular, need to be given this space and freedom. They are not coin-operated machines that can endlessly spit out results. They can produce on demand for a while, but just like any other artist, they need care and feeding.

Giving People Space

If you're a leader, you may be wondering how you can give people time and space to create while also getting things done or keeping a schedule. What is the balance between creative freedom and limits?

It may sound simple here, but it is all about setting up-front expectations. Where can you inject creativity into a project, task, or deliverable? An artist can still push back or try new ideas during the process. However, those will be within tighter constraints up front, which will better keep the work on schedule. A leader can also encourage the artists who are good at execution to encourage the best output from others and help them stay on task.

You can look at the same issue from the artist's perspective. How do you work within boundaries and schedules while maintaining the right creative frame of mind?

The best art comes from some level of constraint. Artists can actually go a bit mad without constraints. For example, look at the Sagrada Família, a cathedral basilica in Barcelona, Spain. It is easily the world's most interesting man-made structure. Designed by the genius architect Antoni Gaudi, the foundation was laid in 1873. The construction of the basilica has never been finished, 140 years after the architect's death.

In the Western world, we practically worship the concept of freedom. Artists don't like limits. But limits and boundaries are the only way to help ensure that creativity is expressed in a form that can be enjoyed or consumed. A canvas has edges, a pop song on the radio has a time limit, and sitcoms are half an hour long. Artful execution can occur when artists know and embrace the timeline or limits of the project.

Although we've covered much ground in this chapter, there is no way to do justice to the depth of the artistic mind in this limited space. Yet, at the same time, isn't that the beauty of artistic thinking? Our minds are like a kaleidoscope of ever-changing shapes and patterns of light. Rather than being an obstacle or a problem to solve, the Business Artist's mind is an essential component of any sales team or business.

Artists think and feel differently than anyone else, particularly when operating in a flow state. In the next chapter, we'll dig more into the specifics of a flow state, why it's essential, and how to experience more of it in your daily life.

8

REACHING A STATE OF FLOW

It's no coincidence that this chapter is the literal center of the book. This is the chapter we have been building toward and the chapter from which everything else will unfold.

In many ways, being a Business Artist is all about *flow*. Without flow, it's difficult to get into the right head space to create art, connect with others, and operate at your highest capacity.

But what is flow, exactly? We have alluded to it in previous chapters, but now it's time to explore this critical element of the artist's life. We'll examine some of the research and benefits of flow, the state of mind where artists do their best work. We'll also examine how to get into a state of flow and consider how my personal experience has shaped my perspective on flow.

Many hardcore business types dismiss the concept of flow. Perhaps it feels like too much of a touchy-feely concept. But I'm here to show you that it's not only a vital part of your creative life—it's also something you can experience for yourself.

Are you ready to flow?

Getting Into a State of Flow

My most memorable experiences of flow have happened when I was challenged or operating at my peak capability. If I'm in front of a large audience giving a speech, I will find ways to work the crowd to pace my content. If I'm doing work that is too repetitive, I'll find ways to innovate. If the work is not challenging or doesn't push my capabilities, I'll flex until I get into the flow.

My experience isn't unique. This is the way many people get into a state of flow. It doesn't happen by accident. You either make the choice to get into flow intentionally, or you are put there by your circumstances.

Many researchers have contributed their ideas on the concept of flow in the last few decades. The most widely accepted model is from Mihaly Csikszentmihalyi's influential 2008 book *Flow: The Psychology of Optimal Experience.*[7] He suggests that flow can be placed at the top right of a chart that marks different emotions based on how they relate to Challenges and Abilities.

For example, you might feel apathetic (sad and depressed) if you don't have many challenges or abilities. You might feel anxious (stressed and alert) if your challenges are high but your abilities are low. Or you might feel relaxed (confident and contented) if your challenges are low but your abilities are high. However, you enter into flow when you have a lot of challenges, but you also have the abilities to handle them well. You are focused and happy.

Mihaly's model is not the only way to look at flow, but it's a wonderful starting point to help us think about the circumstances that can produce a state of flow. When I consider how flow relates to sales, I would argue there is another graphic we could create. Instead of Challenges and Abilities, we could explore Desire and Competence.

Desire refers to questions such as, "Do I want to work with this person? Do I trust them? Are they saying something unique? Do they arouse my curiosity by how they show up in the world?"

Competence refers to questions such as, "Are they good at what they do? Do they believe what they are saying? Has their product or solution worked before? Will it work for me? Is there value I can put in their promise?"

With Desire on the vertical axis and Competence on the horizontal axis, the chart would look like the one below. This could be read from both the buyer's and customer's perspectives.

- High Desire + High Competence (top right)
  = Trust, Impassioned

- High Desire + Low Competence (top left)
  = Concerned, Anxious

- Low Desire + High Competence (bottom right)
  = Serviceable, Reliable

- Low Desire + Low Competence (bottom left)
  = Transactional

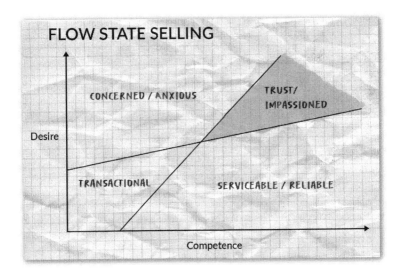

When it comes to getting into a flow state, I'm making a deliberate choice to enter a state of mind where I'm less aware of time. My executive network (the part of my brain that recognizes patterns and drives processes) starts to relax. It feels like I'm falling forward naturally into whatever creative task or unstructured activity is before me. It might be leading a sales kickoff, introducing myself or my solution to a new client, or performing piano for an audience.

No matter what I'm doing, the process always feels the same.

Flow state is a kind of euphoria when I'm at peak performance, maximizing my skills and competence. At the same time, I'm building the desire to see something new. It's not a normal transactional conversation or opportunity. I'm relaxed, not anxious, as I'm entering into a state where I can pick up on disparate information from others. Then, I can quickly draw information from them in a sales meeting, sales kickoff, or virtually any situation.

Flow state is closely related to doing improv. A good improv artist operates in a state of flow when they're in peak performance. The same is true for rappers or jazz musicians. They are no longer thinking. They are doing.

We also see flow in sports. Wayne Gretzky once said he was like a "ghost floating around the ice." He anticipated quickly and positioned himself where the puck was going. Hockey is played so fast and at such a high level that you don't have time to think on the ice.

Muhammad Ali had one of the fastest reaction speeds of any boxer. He would position his body out of harm's way, which made him impossible to hit. He anticipated and reacted in a state of flow.

It's true of any great athlete. They immerse themselves in their performance and see themselves as part of the action, not just one who is watching it. It's why sports continue to draw millions upon millions of people to games and events each year. We're mesmerized by watching athletes in a peak state of flow.

Flow is a big part of music, one of my other passions. Take pianists, for example. They weren't born with fingers that can operate ten times faster. A great pianist can economize their movement. Before they even finish the first movement, they start going to the next position on the keyboard. They see what is going to happen before it needs to happen.

It may sound like magic, but I guarantee it's anything but. Flow isn't just for pro athletes and gifted musicians. It's for everyone.

Where Do You Get Started?

The first thing to realize is that getting into a flow state requires practice and preparation. When you want to enter into flow, you need to create time in your schedule for brainstorming or collaboration. You probably won't just accidentally wind up in flow. You must mentally play out the situation in your head.

Just like any other muscle, your brain has to be warmed up. You don't get up in the morning and start working on your most complicated task three seconds later. You have to wake up, stretch, go for a walk, and perhaps get some coffee. There's a process for getting into an optimal state, and it's a bit different for everyone. Some researchers even suggest waking up and getting into your most high-value task within minutes, as the delta waves of your waking state are closely linked with that of the flow state.

How do you get warmed up in a business setting? I find improv games, micro role-plays, and speaking key parts of my message out loud to be helpful techniques. When I warm up, I don't have to waste my cognitive energy thinking about what I'm going to say, but rather on listening to what is said and unsaid in my meeting.

In a sales meeting, getting into a state of flow begins with solid preparation. Imagine if a jazz musician couldn't riff into improv because they didn't learn the music in advance. I see salespeople all the time, especially in virtual selling, reading PowerPoint notes from a second monitor instead of owning the content, telling a compelling story, and contextualizing it in real time for the customer.

Flow isn't just for the gifted or naturally-born "artists." Flow is within your grasp as long you are willing to prepare and be open to a higher level of thinking.

I don't want you to just take my word for it, though. The science related to flow is well-established. Knowing a bit about how your brain functions will help set a context for thinking about flow. According to psychologist Scott Barry Kaufman, author of the *Scientific American* article "The Real Neuroscience of Creativity," it's helpful to be familiar with three large-scale brain networks if we want to understand the creative process more deeply.[8]

- **Network 1: The Executive Attention Network.** This network kicks into gear when you need to focus your attention on a task like a laser beam.

- **Network 2: The Imagination Network.** When you need to form a mental simulation based on past experiences or thinking about the future, or when you need to imagine what others are thinking, this network answers the call.

- **Network 3: The Salience Network.** This network monitors events happening externally and coordinates them with your internal stream of consciousness to discover the most important information you need at that moment.

You don't need to be a neuroscientist to see that your brain uses different networks for different tasks. For example, Kaufman's article cites research indicating that you should tone down your Executive Attention Network and turn up your Imagination Network if you want to "loosen your associations, allow your mind to roam free, imagine new possibilities, and silence the inner critic…" He also suggests that artists like jazz musicians and rappers do exactly that when improvising in a flow state.

I can't remember a time in school when a teacher told me to take off my thinking cap. But in a sense, that's exactly what we need to do to enter a better state of flow. Sometimes, getting into a flow state means getting out of our own way.

When Your Flow is Blocked

Let's be honest: life doesn't always cooperate with our best intentions to create and innovate. People, events, traffic, your boss, the weather—they can all interfere with your best-laid plans. That's why understanding the obstacles to flow can be helpful.

The place to begin looking for obstacles is not *out there* but *in here.*

Humans have evolved to have the largest prefrontal cortex of any mammal on earth. That is a good thing! The prefrontal cortex controls your thinking, pattern recognition, language, and more. However, it can also prevent you from getting into a flow state.

If you want to try a fun experiment with a friend, play the *opposite game* by giving them a word and asking for the opposite. This will trigger the prefrontal cortex immediately. There's only one problem. Not every word has an opposite. In fact, you could argue that since we invented the word "opposite," there isn't even such thing as the opposite to anything.

Your conversation might go something like this:

What is the opposite of up? *Down.*

What is the opposite of black? *White.*

What is the opposite of red?

Most people will say *green* because red and green are so closely associated with each other at Christmas and are opposite each other on the color wheel (red is primary, green is complementary). They might also say *blue* because of the red-green-blue (RGB) color association.

However, there is no true opposite of red. We took a visible light spectrum and named that range of light *red.* Nature has infrared we can't see, but other insects and animals can see it. They would say the opposite of red is another version of red.

Our ability to get into a flow state is limited by the pattern recognition ("I know the right answer") part of our brain in our prefrontal cortex. We are not comfortable getting into a flow state until the *how-to* part of our brain is satisfied or silenced.

Knowing this, how do artists get past creative roadblocks and back into a state of flow?

I asked my wife, a creative director, how she handles this. She blurted out, "Deadlines!" My own experience confirms she's right. Templates, guides, and other constraining tools can spark great ideas the first few times you use them. However, the template that inspired you will soon hold back new forms of creativity.

Why? Because if you want to operate at your peak, good flow requires time and preparation. But it is so worth it! I love the feeling when I'm truly in a state of flow in a customer meeting. It's remarkable. The trust, confidence, and credibility that shows through on both sides is not only exhilarating, but it always leads to a better and longer-term relationship with the customer. Often, there is time for small personal detours that don't derail but rather add to the cross-connection we have established.

To get into an optimum flow, Business Artists are always seeking ways to quiet the executive network and illuminate the other two networks of the brain to drive new creative thought. This requires a business culture that doesn't just tolerate this approach but celebrates it.

How I Know I'm in a Flow State

For athletes, time slows down when they are in a flow state. The same is true for musicians. Your hand is trying to keep up with your mind. You are no longer thinking; you're just letting go and allowing the flow to take over.

When I'm on stage, I know I'm in flow when I can no longer feel my heart beating or my mind searching for what to do next. It just *does*. I don't think *before* I speak. I think *as* I speak. I'm constantly recalling information from past hours, months, and days, absorbing new information as I filter and analyze like a stock trader on Wall

Street. However, this neural network of processed information isn't an algorithm at work. Rather, it's flow state, and for me, it is beautifully improvised chaos.

It doesn't have to take place on stage, though. It can be a more tactical part of a sales conversation, whether I'm doing discovery, sharing a story, or responding to an objection.

At first, you may feel your body temperature rise as you try to calm the natural defensive response to unpack where this objection is coming from. When I'm in a flow state, though, there is a more heightened relaxation, the conversation slows down, and I'm anticipating instead of reacting to objections. I can read the customer's body language, moving beyond the words they are speaking and trying to identify the root cause. All the while, I'm doing my best to show my empathy and concern before taking the best action to resolution.

Of course, it doesn't have to be a personal interaction. I experience a flow state when I am storyboarding proposals, brainstorming new ideas, or even writing outlines for this book. I'm able to think about what to write and, at the same time, imagine the reaction my audience or customer will have when reading. Words matter, but so does the experience where we want to connect you with the words to identify and recognize pieces of yourself within.

Throughout this book, we've come back to the theme of jazz. It's a wonderful art form for many reasons, one of them being that the creative pathways it takes somehow get mirrored in your brain. There is a certain buoyancy to a lot of jazz music that helps me reflect outward on how a message, idea, or solution will land or be experienced by my customers and audience.

This doesn't work for everyone. For instance, when my wife is doing a brand design, it's all about letting emotions and a mood board guide her in selecting colors, fonts, imagery, copy, and other brand elements. She uses these mood boards as an unconscious filter that helps her start to see and visualize patterns. She'll say, "For a moment, I had mental visualization superpowers!"

In big companies, we focus on output. However, thinking is not about output. You don't get rewarded for thinking. You get rewarded for doing. Email, Slack, and other so-called productivity tools trick us into believing we are doing our job if we are responsive to email and messages. You can see messages and measure them. But it's hard to measure the power of thinking and flow state. Therefore, we don't allow ourselves the opportunity to get there.

That's too bad because getting into a flow state is one of the most important things every Business Artist can do in the bigger picture of improving their business. Let's take a look at a few examples.

Examples of Flow States

In this book, we have primarily talked about business in terms of sales professionals. Although that's been our focus, the concept of a flow state applies to every kind of profession or business, even those you wouldn't normally associate with creativity. Here are a few examples:

- **Attorneys.** The legal field is driven by process and precedent (case law), leaving little room for argument. The Latin *stare decisis* means "to stand by things decided." If a previous court has ruled on a related issue, a court will generally align with previous decision as opposed to setting a new legal precedent.

  While that is true, I have had lawyers tell me that their job is as much about being a Business Artist as any other profession, if not more. They need to argue the law in front of a live audience of a judge and jury. It's not as black and white as the textbooks might imply. Lawyers need to get into a flow state when they are selecting a jury, presenting their case, questioning a witness, performing a cross-examination, or managing a client.

  One lawyer friend told me that taking the law school admission test (LSAT, the test required to get into law school in the US) is nothing like going to law school. Going to law school is nothing like taking the Bar (the exam required to practice law in the US). Taking and passing the Bar is nothing like being an actual lawyer. Each of these steps is about certifying knowledge and being successful in subsequent steps. It requires you to apply your own human knowledge, to adapt, and be agile.

That sounds a lot like being a Business Artist! If you follow the script or process in too much detail, you will never make it as a lawyer.

- **Medical professionals.** You might think of the medical field as bound by strict processes and steps for any given situation. But a surprising amount of intuition, creative thinking, and problem-solving happens in hospitals, emergency rooms, and medical offices every day.

  For example, what happens when all the sensors or data suggest a certain illness or disease, but you must use your instincts to make a different call? Or what about two doctors who disagree on a course of treatment when they both have access to the exact same lab tests and patient history? Doctors performing a diagnosis or treatment have to get creative beyond the scientific method in order to figure out whether you might be lying, giving incomplete information, or being influenced by what you've read online.

  Just a couple of decades ago, doctors didn't have to worry about patients who self-diagnosed by watching YouTube videos. There was a higher degree of patient trust. Now, doctors not only have to deal with patients who believe they know everything (and just want a prescription) but also deal with the complexities and frustrations of the healthcare system.

  No wonder doctors need intuition and creative thinking!

- **Pro athletes.** Although we may not think of professional athletes as businesspeople in a strict sense, they are indeed "in business." You can think of pro sports players as highly paid Business Artists serving customers on a huge scale. They must constantly operate in a flow state.

If you're a football player who has a 250-pound guy chasing you down on the field, you have to make a decision quickly. You can't open a playbook and hope it tells you what to do in the next half second. Because of your intense preparation, you need to let go and operate in a flow state.

We are not robots. Even in professions that operate with lots of protocols and procedures, there is still a measure of latitude. Nearly every job requires some degree of improvisation and quick decision-making. Creative thinking is vital for every profession.

It's All About People

Sometimes, we shrink back from improvising and decision-making because we're afraid of failure. But we can't let the fear of failure ruin us. Jeff Bezos advocates for *productive failure*. You can't prevent failure, but you can always learn from it. Go back to the drawing board and figure out what went wrong, then improve what you're doing.

Many high-level leaders take this approach, where we look at the big picture and spot connections. In addition to Jeff Bezos, thinkers such as Steve Jobs, Elon Musk, and other business innovators have talked about connecting the dots by continuously reading and studying. Whether you're working in finance, biotechnology, or law, all fields become interrelated at some point. This is why studying and learning should be a top priority for every Business Artist.

Flow isn't just about soft skills. It has incredible practical application to the bottom line of business. Why? Because business is all about people. Getting into a flow state can help you in every aspect of sales and human interaction. Is there anything more important than relationships?

9

INNER AND OUTER
CREATIVE FORCES

By this point in the book, I hope you're convinced that the way of the Business Artist is the only path forward. Given the incredible change of pace in today's world, and the fact that you're probably already inclined to think like an artist (after all, you're reading this book!), why would you want to pursue any other path?

All said, being a Business Artist doesn't happen in isolation. The work you do takes place in the real world with real people dealing with real circumstances in real time. One of those "real" factors is the company you work for.

However, there is a natural tension between what you want as an artist and what the company needs. Sales goals, quotas, performance standards, and other metrics need to be met, but it doesn't have to come at the expense of your fulfillment. You spend a pretty good chunk of your life working for a company (or working for yourself). Shouldn't your work give you some level of creative fulfillment while also contributing to the bottom line?

We do our best work when we are fulfilled on multiple levels. But how does that work, especially when your needs as a creative person sometimes collide with the realities of business?

In this chapter, we'll focus on the question, "How can a Business Artist do their best work in a state of flow while also meeting the company's objectives and supporting its bottom line?" These are the internal forces (creative fulfillment) and external forces (company goals) at play.

Let's begin by looking at the delicate balance between creativity and consumption.

Creativity vs. Consumption

In the world of creators (authors, musicians, filmmakers, and painters, to name a few), there is a good deal of discussion about the dangers of consuming too much. All artists know that your creativity works the same way your body does. If you consume too much but don't have enough output, you have serious problems.

But what do we mean by "consumption," exactly? And how do we know when we have done too much of it?

It goes beyond just watching too much Netflix or football. Consumption can also mean consuming your own ideas without challenging them or creating new ideas.

Here's one example. Let's assume I'm talking to a customer. Cognitive friction theory suggests there are three types of memory: sensory, working, and long-term. Sensory memory absorbs information via your five senses (taste, touch, smell, sight, and sound) and hands it to working memory to process or discard it. Most of the new information is discarded.

If I'm meant to hold on to it, my working memory has to categorize, learn, and organize it into some kind of knowledge structure. Then, it is passed on to my long-term memory. All of this requires a great deal of cognitive effort and energy.

As my customer is talking, I'm waiting for them to say something that triggers or tempts my brain to "relax" and share some information like product details or an old story that may or may not relate to them.

It's easier for you and me to share something we've already consumed and can recall instead of trying to stay present and create something new.

This isn't due to a lack of effort or desire. We only have so much capacity in our working memory. Have you ever had too many apps open on your computer, causing it to freeze? Your working memory functions the same way. There is only so much new information you can add at a time.

Because of this, we look for ways to help our brains relax and avoid getting overloaded. But the more you fall into this pattern, the more you miss opportunities to train your working memory. Thus, it becomes harder to get into a flow state and create new connections with your customers.

The inner force of a limited amount of working memory is a constant battleground where we have to expand our ability to retain new information. But it's not the only place where conflict happens. There are a few other battlegrounds that threaten creative thinking, one of which is the pressure to conform.

Creativity vs. Conformity

Before starting Meahana, I spent thirteen years building and deploying simulations with the goal of helping clients become better businesspeople and sales leaders. I've modeled various situations with clients and their executive teams many times. The basic question always comes down to this: How do customers and employees feel about the value of creativity?

The weighting of this answer is determined by the company (market leader, niche player, or new entrant) as well as the market growth rate of the segment (mature slow growth, medium, or hyper-growth).

Not surprisingly, new entrants put a premium on creativity. Why? Because customers demand creativity and it helps fuel a company's early growth. As companies and market segments mature, the "value of creativity" erodes as the focus shifts to building processes and increasing scale.

Even if you're not innovating on the product or customer side, you can still function as a Business Artist when it comes to being more efficient or helping employees stay engaged. For example, what if you could invent a new way for people to share information or create knowledge communities in a way that doesn't feel *corporate* but instead feels authentic and helps people build new relationships?

Or what if you could develop an innovative way to test and iterate new product ideas that involve not just the product team itself but also individuals from across the business? You would get a much more diverse range of ideas and opinions, therefore increasing the chance you would spot design flaws earlier in the process.

This all sounds great and, of course, everyone wants to have better products earlier in the design process. That helps everyone. But how do you actually build a bridge between creativity and conformity? I believe the answer lies in a scientific approach.

There is an artistic way to do a task, which at first is focused on finding new approaches, seeking out divergent thinking, and keeping the brain in exploration mode. This goes on until the artist sees a pathway forward or they discover a certain routine that can become a process.

At that point, no more iteration is required. The brain sits back and says, "*For now*, this is the new way of doing this task, this workflow, this type of customer slide deck." And the brain is able to then focus on new creative tasks. The ones completed *for now* are put into a standardization framework and often distributed to others so they can also conform.

This happens all the time in new businesses and organizations. At first, there aren't many official *policies*. There is usually no employee handbook, no complicated HR department, and rules and regulations are kept to a minimum. But as time goes on, the team grows, and you encounter various situations that set precedents; the list of standardized practices keeps growing and growing.

Over time, you find as an artist that it's hard to be creative in your work because everything involves levels of red tape that crush your enthusiasm and make you wonder if it's worth the effort in the first place.

So, how can you move forward? I propose that the balance between creativity and conformity must exist on the following framework:

The question to ask is: "Is this a task that would benefit from a Business Artist approach?"

- If yes, would this task need a new approach regularly or infrequently?

- If regularly, this is not a good task for developing conformity.

- If infrequently, a conformist approach may work for a while.

- If no, a conformist approach should work for a while.

Here's one small example: introducing yourself at the start of a sales meeting. Is this a task that would benefit from a Business Artist approach? Yes, of course. This is a task that needs a new approach regularly. Therefore, this is not a good task for conformity to be developed.

Here's why: The Business Artist seller would never expect themselves or anyone else to use a canned introduction script. Instead, they would sculpt a new talk based on the people in the meeting and the vibe, making sure to connect with everyone and create a memorable experience.

Before we come down to the idea of conformity too hard, though, it's important to understand that conformity is not necessarily a bad thing. In fact, it's a vital part of any group or organization that is going to get anything done over the long term. The opposite of conformity is anarchy. A collection of people all doing their own thing and rebelling against any sense of control is obviously unhealthy unless you want daily riots and protests on your hands!

A 2012 study from Harvard Business Review (HBR) showed that conformity is a key component of a creative culture. You need creative types (aka Business Artists) on your team, but you need other cognitive types—namely, conformists.

They wrote, "We studied forty-one radical innovation teams. The groups had varying proportions of three types of people—extremely creative, detail-oriented, and highly conformist—along with more general thinkers, typically the largest component. Our most surprising finding: Conformists, though they may be useless at generating breakthrough ideas, dramatically increase a team's radical innovations."[9]

The bottom line is that creativity and conformity are not at odds— they are bedfellows in the pursuit of innovation. You need a good balance of both approaches.

Exercises for Getting into a Flow State

As artists, we are quick to desire a state of flow. But I think it's important to first answer what prevents us from developing a better, longer, more intense flow state.

The answer, as crazy as it sounds, is that we inadvertently think our way out of it. We focus on one thought instead of letting several play out at the same time. It may just be that our overactive mind needs a break. It's burning more energy than normal in a flow state, and just like our muscles build up lactic acid when they get fatigued, so does our brain when it is hyperactive.

I'll give you an example. Say you are holding a tennis ball, throwing it up in the air, and catching it. You can do this for hours. But what about two balls? How about when you are juggling three, now five, balls?

At this point, you can no longer think of any one ball. If you focus on just one, even for a second, you'll drop all of them. If you've ever watched jugglers, their eyes are looking directly forward. They have trained themselves to have muscle memory to know and react to every slight miss.

Just as a juggler can learn to throw more objects and do more tricks, so can your brain with the right games or exercises. The key to this is similar to learning how to be great at discovery and storytelling. You must have lots of practice, repetition, and immersion.

Let me suggest some exercises for getting into a flow state. Here's an improv game I enjoy leading with a group. Start with each person saying a word in a sentence:

Person A: "Once"

Person B: "upon"

Person C: "a time," etc.

Eventually, let people do full sentences before turning them over to the next person. When it takes someone a long time to respond, they are *dropping the ball* and are not in a flow state. Do it again with sales colleagues and build a collaborative improv story of a customer who needs your product.

Here's another game where you break into groups of three. You get thirty seconds to introduce yourself or your product to a customer. The next person takes the information they just heard and plays it back in fifteen seconds or less. The last person takes just ten seconds to introduce the product or person.

This game will be impossible for many sellers at first. Thirty seconds will never seem like enough time, but by the end, the product pitch or personal elevator introduction will be crisp, tight, and memorable.

These activities are designed to get individuals into a flow state by helping them move away from overthinking and perfectionism. It presumes that people are operating from a place of energy and engagement to begin with. How can we set up ourselves, and our teams, for success in their mental, physical, and emotional well-being to optimize flow?

The Role of Health and Wellness

In previous decades, there was a much bigger emphasis on doing "whatever it takes" to get the job done. You might recall movies like

Glengarry Glen Ross or *Wall Street*, which showed us what happens in the business world when people decide to "win" at all costs. They not only sacrifice their integrity but, in some cases, also destroy their mental and physical health.

All our talk about creativity, flow, and innovation is wonderful, but those have to happen within physical bodies that get tired and need proper hydration, rest, nutrition, and exercise. We can't ignore the impact of health and wellness on our ability to get into flow and be effective Business Artists.

A professional athlete rests their muscles before the competition. They also make sure to get enough sleep. When we sleep, we experience cognitive restoration along with the restoration of our bodies.

Amazon founder Jeff Bezos has an almost religious belief about the importance of sleep. His perspective is that the higher up you go in a company, the less work you do, and the number of big decisions you make each day increases. There's more at stake, so you must be at your best.

During a discussion at the Economic Club of Washington in 2018, he spoke about the importance of sleep. He reflected, "I think better. I have more energy. My mood is better."[10] Bezos is very calculative about why he believes eight hours of sleep is the key to boosting productivity and making high-quality decisions.

In addition, a 2017 study published in the Annals of Neurology discovered that your decision-making is impaired when you don't get enough sleep.[11] This is only the very tip of the iceberg since a massive number of studies have been done on the mind-body connection.

It cannot be over-stated enough how much sleep, diet, and exercise play into your physical energy, mental mood, and motivation for being an effective artist and leader.

I can always feel when I'm "off." I'm less patient, more irritable, and end up going through the motions. I have to shift my energy to compensate in certain bursts throughout the day. It's dreadful to know you're not at your best, but we all have these days or moments. It's equally important to know how to match the energy of your customers or colleagues.

As we explore the topic of energy and its connection to creativity and a state of flow, it's worth considering how corporate wellness programs can help employees stay healthy. With massive cultural crises in obesity, mental health, and more, companies have paid much more attention to this area in recent years.

It's hard to argue with a company that might take the viewpoint of personal responsibility—employees are responsible for their health and well-being. However, I believe any company serious about getting the best cognitive output from its employees should do whatever it can to promote and educate about the benefits of health and wellness, but not require it.

There has been an explosion of companies and resources available in this space. A colleague of mine, Matt Prostko, left BTS to initially run sales and now heads up Products for TaskHuman, a company that connects employees and individuals with one-on-one sessions to promote wellness. These sessions can involve scheduling a yoga teacher, nutritionist, sound healer, sleep therapist, or someone to lead you in guided meditation, all the way to more career-focused areas like sales and leadership coaching.

It's a great company that sees the value in the mind-body connection and found a way to make services affordable, scalable, and, most importantly, on-demand. Any Business Artist can schedule a session when convenient or when they feel like they need it. I have personally experimented with guided meditation sessions just before I needed to do some heavy creative work. It helps to remove the rest of the day's *mental debris* that will cloud the blank slate and the focus I will need.

As you've made your way through this chapter, I hope it has sparked some ideas about how you can navigate the forces that can keep us from unleashing our full *flow* potential. Before we move on to the final chapter of Part 2, I want to address a challenge many Business Artists have faced, particularly since the COVID-19 pandemic.

The Challenge of Working from Home

Everything we have talked about so far in the book can be applied to people working from home, just in different ways. We all know that being present in a group work environment brings certain interpersonal dynamics that can't be replicated when you're working at home. But that doesn't make one good and the other bad. They're just different, each with their own set of challenges.

When you work from home, you don't have the chance to collaborate with people in person, but you typically have more time and headspace. There are always trade-offs.

If there is one thing that the pandemic has taught us, it is that people are vastly different, and they each like to work in their own way. I've been in several large client leadership meetings where they discussed their approaches to bringing people back to work. One of the concepts I've pushed is the value of in-office time for building relationships. No one is doubting that. Relationships, particularly new relationships among colleagues, have suffered.

The pandemic took away certain opportunities for a while, but it also brought new ones. Many people had never worked from home before. They now had more free time and the chance to operate in a new work setting.

We had new constraints. For people with creative minds, new constraints meant time to go to work, solve problems, and create new ways of working. That's exactly what I did. Even before the pandemic, I realized that technology often fails to tap into our inherent potential for creativity and innovation. Traditional collaboration tools aren't exceptions.

This is where Meahana shines. We designed our platform to cultivate a flow state of collaboration, enabling teams to *think together better* and harness the power of their collective wisdom.

Collaboration was what I missed the most during the pandemic. I live on the energy of new relationships and human connections. When that went away, my mood went from positive to negative, and my creative capacity followed suit until I could find new ways to fill the gap.

But isn't that the story of creativity in a nutshell? Humans get used to an unavoidable reality—things change, and we adjust. In the process, we find new and interesting ways of working. The newness opens opportunities that we never had before. It also shuts off old opportunities, and we sometimes mourn those old ways of working and being. That is the push and pull of the Business Artist, those inner and outer creative forces we have to face every day.

In the end, why do we do all this? Why strive for more creativity? What's the end result?

It's about our creative expression, of course, but it's more than that. If you're using your artistry in the workplace, there's another priority at stake. Every business ultimately exists to serve the customer or client. In the next chapter, we'll see how the creative forces we've been talking about can be put to use not just to sell products and services but to make every single customer a hero.

10

THE CUSTOMER IS THE HERO

As you've already noticed, storytelling is one of the themes I have interwoven into this book the most. I have used stories to try to engage you as the reader, but I've also done my best to show the power of storytelling in the sales process.

There's another way to use storytelling to help us become better Business Artists. That is by looking at the most important relationship in any story: the one between the mentor and the hero. As a salesperson, it is easy to see yourself as the hero, the center of the story. It feels like you're the one doing all the work, trying to close the deal and please several parties in the process, including the customer, your manager, your colleagues, and ultimately yourself.

I want to challenge your thinking here. You are not the hero of the sales story. The customer is. If so, what role are you playing as the salesperson? The mentor.

In any good story, the hero has a character arc that shows how they have changed or learned a lesson. Your goal in sales is to help the customer be more successful by taking your recommendation or buying what you're selling.

Looking at sales through this lens takes the pressure off of having to "convince" the customer to buy. Instead, you become the mentor who invites the customer to join you on a transformative journey.

Salespeople are taught to use different strategies to address customers' objections or convince them to buy. But none of us is really selling a service or product. What we are selling is a life change. Who better to help the customer experience change than a mentor who is there to guide them along the journey?

You don't have to be the strongest, wisest, or smartest person in the room to be a mentor. You just need something of value to offer and a willingness to lead the way. You're the Alfred to their Batman, the Gandalf to their Frodo, the Obi-Wan to their Luke.

It doesn't mean you have to know everything. In fact, all true artists are both teaching and learning at the same time. One of the hallmarks of a great mentor is that they are always learning. Mentors and students collaborate, critique, and sometimes compete with each other. They respect each other's gifts and enjoy being challenged.

A Lesson from Leonardo

Business Artists can be great mentors. But artists also *need* a mentor. Think of some of the great artistic minds from the past few decades. Whitney Houston had record executive Clive Davis. Michael Jackson had producer Quincy Jones. Steven Spielberg had movie mogul Sid Sheinberg. Every great artistic mind has a mentor.

Sometimes, the mentor does such a fine job that the student and mentor swap roles. If properly taught, a good student can grow into a great teacher.

This is exactly what happened with Leonardo da Vinci. As a student in Florence in the late fifteenth century, he eclipsed his teacher Verrocchio with his contribution to the *Baptism of Christ*. This painting combined clay, terra, and watercolor with an oil painting style.

Leonardo's contribution was so skillful that Verrocchio supposedly resolved never to paint again.

Leonardo did the exact opposite. Instead of shrinking his creative canvas, he expanded it. As a young artist still in his twenties, he continued not just to use oil but also experimented with all sorts of mediums as he grew in his skill and confidence.

Leonardo's approach is a beautiful expression of what it means to be an artist. He wasn't just concerned about the end product. He became a student of science, nature, medicine, warfare, engineering, and other areas. Even in his lifetime, he was known as one of the greatest creative minds in history because of his interdisciplinary approach to art and learning.

In sales, we often do the opposite by focusing on the end result instead of the process. If your customer gets mediocre results from your product or service, but you are proud of your *sale* and the commission, you are missing the point. You are not the hero. Instead, your role is to *enable* the hero (the customer) to be successful.

This is one of the most important functions of the Business Artist. But how exactly do you make the customer the hero? Turns out you can't do it by yourself. It requires a team of collaborators who can complement each other's skills to deliver the best possible experience to the customer.

The Business of Creativity

As kids, we are not often taught in school to take creativity seriously. You might have dabbled in painting with watercolor in grade school, played a role in a high school theater production, or taken an art course in college. Experiences like those were probably seen as *extras* in the curriculum.

Subjects like art, music, and theater have taken a backseat to left-brained pursuits like science, engineering, and math. We don't encourage kids to consider careers in art or music. Our intentions are good. We don't want our kids to become *starving artists*. Yet, in trying to protect them, we have missed the truth that creativity is, in fact, *big business.*

Every business involves creative thinking on some level. At its core, creativity is about problem-solving, and you can't have a successful business without solving problems. However, some industries involve more traditional creative expression while simultaneously serving a huge number of customers and making boatloads of money in the process. Let me give you two examples.

First is a typical record company. They sell records (the product) to fans (the customers). The record company employs recording artists, singers, studio musicians, producers, and engineers to create the finished product (the songs and albums).

To create this product, an immense amount of artistic collaboration is required, often pulling from different areas of musical and technical expertise. And in today's music world, where hit singles are more important than ever, artists will recruit a whole team of songwriters to craft just the right songs (which may or may not hit the mark since a hit single is never guaranteed).

But creating the actual product is only the first step. Now the marketing team has to promote the record, and the sales team must sell the *packaged product* to stores (retail and online partners who resell it at a profit) or streaming services (who give the record company a cut of the profit).

The next time you turn on the radio or open your music streaming app, remember how many people, how much creative effort, and how many business decisions have gone into creating that one song. (We haven't even mentioned video production or social media.)

Second, let's look at a software company, with a surprisingly similar workflow as a record company. They sell software (the product) to users or subscribers (the customers). Software companies employ engineers and other personnel to first create the product. For this to happen, an immense amount of artistic collaboration is required, often pulling in from different areas of expertise just like a record company does. Except in this case, we're talking about the product owner, the project manager, software developers, UX/UI designers, the team lead, the tech lead, the scrum master, and others.

Once the product is created, the marketing team promotes it, and the sales team sells it to retail locations or online stores. Increasingly, they are selling directly to customers and creating software that requires a subscription.

I've shared all this to point out that many people are involved in the creation of a great artistic product. Although the world of music is known as "the arts," there is always a large team around a hugely successful artist. One of Taylor Swift's recent albums had eight writers, twenty-four musicians, and twenty-six technical engineers! To maintain that level of success, she has to collaborate and take input from many different people.

The same is true for software companies as well. Although individual "superstars" are not as common in the software field, you know exactly what these companies make: Adobe, Salesforce, IBM, and Microsoft, to name a few. Even though you're familiar with their product, you'd be hard-pressed to name even one developer who worked on those products. But those individuals are still artists using their creativity for the good of others, especially when they are working in teams.

The People Behind the Products

When you use a product, you don't normally think about the people who created it. You play the song, turn on the coffeemaker, start the car, or ask your phone what time it is. Go throughout your day and stop to consider how the products you use actually came into being. You'll have a new sense of appreciation for the entrepreneurs, artists, and designers who brought them to life.

Consider Steve Jobs and Steve Wozniak, Larry Page and Sergey Brin, or Bill Gates and Paul Allen. If you've ever used an Apple product, searched using Google, or created a document with Microsoft Office, you have been impacted by partnerships that changed the world.

One of my favorite business partnerships is Ben Cohen and Jerry Greenfield, of Ben and Jerry's ice cream. Why does their partnership work? Because they were able to turn their friendship into a successful business thanks to a joint passion for food and a desire to create more than just profit.

The pair are adamant about giving back to the community, which resonates with their customers. Greenfield has said, "We measured our success not just by how much money we made, but by how much we contributed to the community. It was a two-part bottom line."[12] What other business leader besides these two could give us such creative ice cream flavors like Chunky Monkey and Cherry Garcia?

What if we had the same level of reverence for other artists in the business world? You might like drinking Casamigos Tequila because George Clooney owns it, but do you know who the master distiller is? Or perhaps you know Ryan Reynolds is part owner of Aviation Gin, but do you know where or how it's made?

It's useful for popular brands to have a celebrity who can promote it. Marketing is important! But let's not forget about the Business Artists who design, develop, create, promote, and sell these products we use and love. The people who create things we use aren't just a faceless mob. They are real people who have worked hard and collaborated to bring you these products.

If you really want to know why you like something, find out how it was created. But don't stop there. Bring the same curiosity to your business or workplace. Who actually creates the products you sell? Showing appreciation for the creative nuances of great products and the people who create them will give you insights you've never had before. You'll see new patterns emerge that will influence your ability to operate like a Business Artist.

Companies don't create art. People do. I really believe that. Companies should profit from the artists they employ, but in our brand-driven culture, we have lost touch with the human beings who make the things we use and love, whether it's spirits, ice cream, software, music, or any other consumer item.

In the sales process, the customer is the hero. You are the guide and mentor. But the customer isn't the only hero. The men and women who give their creative efforts to create the product you sell? They don't usually get recognized, but they're also heroes and should be treated as such.

This brings us to a controversial question that ignites a heated debate among writers, artists, and creatives of every kind: giving credit to your collaborators.

How This Book Was Created

I've noted that Taylor Swift uses a team of musicians, writers, and engineers to produce her music. It takes all of them to bring you the music you hear on streaming or the radio.

The same is true for the book you're reading. I was not the sole author of *The Business Artist*. I worked with a ghostwriter, Kent Sanders, to flesh out the concept, outline the book, and actually write the book. Kent is a full-time ghostwriter and an author in his own right. He also hosts a podcast called *The Profitable Writer* and runs a membership group for writers called The Profitable Writer Community, which focuses on helping writers earn a living with their skills.

Kent and I connected through our mutual friend, Andy Storch, a Talent Development expert, author, speaker, and trainer. When I started working with Kent, I told him from the beginning that one of the themes of *The Business Artist* was collaboration, and therefore, I wanted to publicly credit him as the book's ghostwriter.

Ghostwriting can work in many different ways, depending on the project, the writer, and the author. Sometimes, the author (the person named on the book's cover—in this case, me) is very involved in the book's creation. Other times, the ghostwriter takes a germ of an idea and runs with it, with the named author not having much creative input.

In the case of this book, Kent and I worked together closely to create a finished version of the book ready for editing and publishing. We had regular calls to talk about the contents of each chapter. Then Kent would record them to produce a written transcript. He also sent dozens of prompts to spur my thinking. I would either write out my responses or create voice recordings.

Then, Kent created drafts of each chapter. We worked together to refine the content. In addition, we had many other collaborators since I recruited a team of beta readers who gave valuable insights and feedback at every step of the book creation process. The book would have been much weaker if not for these friends and colleagues who took the time to help.

The concept of "ghost collaborators" is not unique to the world of books. There are ghost producers in music as well. Listen to the song *Nightcall* by the artist Kavinsky. If you've seen the Ryan Gosling movie *Drive*, you'll recognize that song from the opening scene. If you're a music fan, you might notice something eerily familiar about its style, tonality, and production. With a couple of Google clicks, you'll discover that it was, in fact, produced by Thomas Bangalter and Guy-Manuel de Homem-Christo (better known as the legendary duo *Daft Punk*). If you research a little further, you'll discover that they have ghost-produced tons of tracks from iconic artists.

When you discover that a track was ghost-produced by an artist you're familiar with, listen closely. You'll hear a meshing of styles different from the ghost producer's and artist's styles. Yet it's also familiar because it's mixing the two.

That's how ghostwriting works. Kent spent countless hours assessing my voice memos and transcripts of our calls to understand my voice. The main ideas in the book are all mine, but the production of them into a coherent narrative you're reading now is where I needed his expertise.

Most music producers get credit on the album, but that's not true of most ghostwriters. They will sometimes negotiate for a "with" credit, meaning their name is in smaller print under the author's name on the book cover. But sometimes, they are not credited in a book at all. If they are, it's usually indicated by a generic reference in the Acknowledgments section as someone who "helped bring this book to life," or "assisted with the content," or "provided editorial help."

Most ghostwriters don't care about getting credit because they're primarily concerned with making a living by their trade. However, I strongly disagree with the notion of not giving credit to people who strongly influence creative work. Hence, that's why Kent's name is on the cover, and why I encourage the practice of using ghostwriters who can help you create the book you've been thinking about for years.

The Business Artist at work, no matter what their role, is always giving credit to their collaborators. It's what allows the business ecosystem to thrive. It doesn't diminish your brand to work with collaborators, use a ghostwriter, or get help. It says the opposite. When you acknowledge your collaborators, you say to the world, "I'm smart enough to stick with my strengths and get expert help to make my product the best it can be."

Co-Opetition: Collaboration on the Next Level

The best Business Artists don't just look for partners outside of their core market. They also look *inside* their market for competitors who can partner with them to create a strategic win/win for both parties.

In the HBO documentary *Spielberg*, famed director Steven Spielberg recounts his early days as a movie director. He was friends with a group of young directors who would all become legendary: George Lucas, Francis Ford Coppola, Brian DePalma, and Martin Scorsese. Sometimes, they collaborated with one another. For instance, Lucas helped Coppola by editing the famous montage sequence in *The Godfather* featuring newspaper headlines, DePalma suggested to Lucas that he begin *Star Wars* with a text crawl like the ones featured in old-time movie serials, and Spielberg and Lucas collaborated on the Indiana Jones movies.

They wanted each other's movies to be good, but not *too* good. It was a game of friendly competition where each drove the others to greater success.

In the business world, how do you figure out whether you should collaborate with a partner who might seem to be your competitor? This might work in the movie business, where people can see lots of movies and are *customers* to many different directors and studios. But how does it work when you are considering a partnership with a company that's a direct or indirect competitor, and your customer isn't going to buy the same thing from both of you?

In these cases, you focus on the principle of the *net value of collaboration*. Here's a simple formula to break it down:

Collaboration Value > (Collaboration Costs + Opportunity Costs)

For example, when SAP (the market leader in enterprise application software) does an enterprise resource planning (ERP) integration, it must commit a team of developers to the project for several months. Integration is the process of connecting your company's software to other applications for greater efficiency. While this may sound like a net win, there is actually an opportunity cost to devoting resources to these integrations. The reason is that you have to sacrifice client-facing consulting and engineering time, which directly affects revenue.

Ultimately, when the collaboration value of integrations outweighs the costs, SAP can then offer clients a suite of accessibility that was otherwise impossible. But it required a sacrifice on the front end of the process.

Co-opetition is becoming increasingly important for sellers to understand and embrace as they build relationships. COVID-19 ushered in a new age of remote work and the acceleration of the gig economy. Companies don't need to have all the capability (or their employees) under one roof to succeed. They need to have a network of capabilities and know how to contract with them at the right terms to create the most value for their customers and the marketplace.

I remember when Skype came on the horizon. I made great use of this video communication platform, created by a Scandinavian company, from the mid-2000s to 2014 to call back home when I traveled abroad. You probably used it, too. We would say, "Skype me when you get there." It was such a ubiquitous tool that even corporations used it.

Then, a company named Microsoft bought Skype. However, they stopped investing in it and turned it into an enterprise communication tool that only worked well for existing Microsoft shops. You could use it to share a Microsoft Office file, but no other competing products outside their closed ecosystem. As a result, other companies got into the game. You've probably used more than one of these: Join.Me, GoToMeeting, Webex, or AdobeConnect.

They all gained traction until Slack came along and impressed everyone with its rapid growth. I remember doing a sales workshop for Slack when they only had thirty sellers. We were workshopping their sales process, looking to define the most critical moments in a customer life cycle, from discovery through purchase, to implementation and renewal.

There was something very different about working with Slack. They had an open ecosystem and partner mindset from the beginning. They didn't see themselves as simply a communication platform at all. Instead, they seemed intent on being a workflow platform where anyone can use them as the conduit to get work done.

Do you want to drop in a Google note, not a Microsoft one? No problem. Don't want to use our video, but instead drop in a Zoom meeting invite? Go for it. Don't want to log into your CRM to tag new sales activity? You can do it right here. This latter functionality encouraged Salesforce to spend a whopping $28 billion to acquire the company in 2020, the most expensive subscription software acquisition of all time, paying twenty-six times Slack's forward revenue.

Time will tell how that deal will play out. It has been a rocky start, reportedly due to clashing company cultures. Culture plays a *huge* role in driving acquisitions. Culture and relationships are especially important when we're talking about coming together as a sales team.

Collaboration in the Sales Process

Let's go back to our music metaphor. You'll get this if you have heard a live jazz ensemble playing. There is always a break where the instruments stop the melody and hum through the chord progression while allowing another instrument to *solo* for a bit. It's remarkable. With no verbal communication, the jazz players carry on, trusting each other and playing their part, even though there is an element of improvisation.

This works well most of the time. But sometimes, you'll have a musician who gets impatient with how the soloist is performing. They want to jump in with their own solo, throwing the other musician out of the spotlight.

Egos are now involved, and the music loses some of the magic because they are competing, not cooperating. They've lost trust and have created a micro-culture of suspicion. The other bandmates seem confused, yet they play on, hoping for a musical (and emotional) resolution.

When you've lost trust, it's awfully hard to function as a team. That's just as true in business as it is in music. Selling is not just an exchange of products and services for money. A relationship is involved between the seller (you) and the customer (the hero). In team selling, your relationships with your colleagues are just as important.

There is always an art and a science to selling, especially team selling. The science piece is finite and guided by constraints such as what your solution is or isn't, how much you are allowed to negotiate, or what is required internally for a deal to advance from one stage to the next. Team selling is about knowing the different team roles, their areas of expertise, and how to utilize them in a sales process.

The art piece comes from the real-world improvisational skills that are required. At SAP, one of the more strategic workshops I helped create and run was around team collaboration and team selling. The focus was not so much on up-front sales but more on driving consumption of SAP solutions over the long term. For their largest accounts, this means many specialized resources being brought in at the right time across the customer lifecycle.

Leading the process is a global account director (GAD). This person plays a kind of quarterback role running the team, including several solution and industry account executives, pre-sales solution architects, and industry value engineers. This group is responsible for shaping the total deal, which includes discovery, showing demonstrations, building a business case, and any technical validation. Then, they partner with a second team focused more on adoption and consumption over a long period of time. This second team includes individuals such as customer success, services, and other internal and external partners as needed.

Everyone on this extended account team (collectively called a VAT) has a specific role. But more importantly, they each need to know each other's role, area of expertise, and how to utilize them in the sales process.

The role I haven't mentioned but is likely the most important is the customer. The group I mentioned above has to constantly be in step with what the customer seeks at each step of their collaboration.

I liken this to a piano where each member of the SAP VAT is a white key. The song they play doesn't always go "do, re, mi, fa, so, la, ti, do" until there is success. Sales isn't that linear anymore. Maybe it never was. The customer wants it sped up or slowed down, or two or three notes need to be played simultaneously. This requires some level of improvising.

Glenn Wallace, the GAD for the Lockheed Martin account, recently announced a new twenty-five-year partnership with SAP. He said it best: "We've been working as an account team for so long, we know and appreciate the strengths each brings. Sometimes, we are all doing parts of the team roles, depending on the customer's need at that time. It takes a lot of trust, improvising, and shared accountability."

This doesn't happen overnight. And just like most of my clients, there are team frameworks that lay out an ideal way to operate. It's good to have sheet music to study and learn, but you also have to give yourself permission to improvise by focusing on what the customer needs.

As sales has evolved in complexity, the need for team selling has increased in almost every organization I've encountered. Collaborating with other team members for their expertise is no longer a *nice to have*. It has become essential. Despite this, many sellers maintain a hero mentality and don't correctly apply an artistic approach toward bringing in the right collaborators at the right time and mutually trusting each other. Organizations also fumble this up by being too rigid when putting together a process to create teams.

After all, the only way to make the customer the hero is by performing heroic acts of teamwork, selflessness, and collaboration. As we move into Part 3 of the book, we'll further break down this pathway and offer practical ways to make this a reality in your organization.

PART 3

HARMONY

HOW BUSINESS ARTISTS
CAN MAKE A DIFFERENCE

11

CARING FOR THE CREATOR

Throughout this book, I've tried to bring a mix of principles, practical strategies, and ideas to help you get a sense of the biggest problems facing business leaders today. We've identified three of those primary problems: imitation, perception, and automation. No matter what type of business you're in, you have undoubtedly seen these factors at work in your company or industry.

At its core, this book is about relationships. We think of business as something *out there*—a force outside of ourselves. But business is *you*. Business is *me*. Business is just an agreed-upon system where we add value to one another to create products and services that enhance our lives.

Going back to the metaphor I introduced at the beginning of the book, relationships are like jazz. Just like a good melody can meander in and out of a jazz tune, there is an ebb and flow to relationships. We have endless opportunities for mixing and re-mixing as our relationships evolve. Just like jazz often circles back to the main theme at the end, we keep returning to the central theme of *The Business Artist*: relationships.

With that in mind, here in Part 3, we will focus on five different levels of relationships as we try to navigate the accelerating change all around us. If we don't figure out how to lean into the wind, it will inevitably knock us down. In the next few chapters, we'll talk about navigating change in five concentric circles, each one expanding outward into the next. These are the circles we operate in as Business Artists, and we need to be proficient at each one.

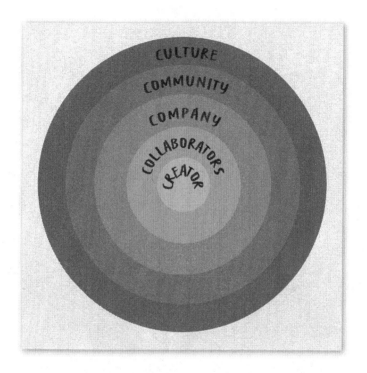

In this chapter, we begin with the smallest circle in the middle: the Creator. In other words, you! It's easy to look *out there* for solutions to the world's problems, but you can't control what others do. You can influence others but you do not control them.

In the landmark book, *The 7 Habits of Highly Effective People*, Dr. Stephen Covey wrote about the differences between your "circle of influence" and your "circle of concern."[13] Your circle of concern is much larger than your circle of influence. Why? Because you're naturally concerned about many different things. You're worried about things happening at the world, national, state, local, and neighborhood levels. That's human nature.

Your circle of influence is much smaller than your circle of concern. You don't control the world, but you do have a lot of influence on a few things. If you're a business owner, entrepreneur, or leader, you have a significant amount of influence because of your role.

Ultimately, the only entity you truly control is yourself. That's why, in this chapter, we will begin by focusing on what you can do to develop as a Business Artist. How do you care for yourself as a Creator?

The source of all innovation is people. People are the source of everything good in our lives. Therefore, if we want to relate well to the rest of the world, we must start with how we relate to ourselves. You can't hate yourself and still be a good Business Artist. As a result, this chapter will address several self-care issues related to your mental health, cognition, sleep, and more.

Your Mental Health

We haven't addressed issues related to mental health much in the book so far, but I'd like to take a portion of this chapter to focus on this vital topic. It's not only an important theme all over the world today, but it's also a key component of self-care. How can we stay mentally healthy as Business Artists?

The word health comes from the old English *hælth*, which means wholeness, being whole, or being sound. Today, we still often refer to health as physical health. However, if we consider what it really means to be whole—to be sound and to be well—we have to include mental health in that definition.

As a Business Artist, to be healthy means you are physically well, but also takes into consideration your emotional, psychological, and social well-being. As someone who has struggled with mental health, I know how important it is to feel balanced and sane and to be at your best for yourself and others.

For many, art is a useful form of psychotherapy. Creativity is a way to express yourself, and it's known to improve your mood, reduce anxiety and depression, and increase self-esteem. I wonder, though, if conditions like anxiety or depression can actually be a part of the value we bring to the world. Could they be useful in some way?

For example, Abraham Lincoln famously struggled with his *melancholy*, and he wouldn't have been the same president if that had been removed from his personality. Or what about Van Gogh's depression, which you could argue contributed to his artistic greatness? At what point do you accept something as part of your makeup instead of trying to medicate it?

On the other side of the argument, we have to keep in mind that not everyone with anxiety or depression will become a great leader or artist. There is a risk in romanticizing mental health issues as being somehow necessary or even desirable for achieving success. It can also create a stigma against seeking treatment.

I would never encourage someone to avoid treatment because they believe it will "take away their artistry." As someone who has been diagnosed with bipolar disorder and has been treated for it, my life has improved, and my ability to be creative and artistic is more focused, more deliberate, and less chaotic.

I'm not attempting to give medical advice that should be reserved for professionals. However, my purpose here is simply to get you to become more aware of mental health's role in your life.

There is still an unfortunate stigma around admitting that you have a mental health struggle. People might judge you as somehow less capable or deficient. Nothing could be further from the truth. You wouldn't consider taking someone out of the running for a job just because they had celiac disease or were diabetic. And neither should we penalize people who have mental health struggles.

Most of all, I don't want you to penalize or punish yourself. My goal is to create more awareness of mental health here and encourage you to give it the attention it deserves in your life.

Mental Health and Self-Awareness

It is easy to talk about the importance of mental health or perhaps give various tips on improving it. But that's not very helpful unless you have some measure of self-awareness of how you're wired, how you work, and how you relate with others. When you really understand who you are, you can better see your blind spots, those areas where you need partners and collaborators.

There are loads of "type assessments" out there: Strengths Finder, Myers-Briggs, Enneagram, DiSC, Four Color Personalities, and the Goleman emotional quotient (EQ) test, among many others. You have probably taken one or more of these yourself. Let me offer a few thoughts on how to use assessments to understand yourself better, enhance your mental health, and ultimately become a stronger Business Artist.

My first piece of advice is that you shouldn't take any assessment too literally. It's meant to uncover how you process life, work, and relationships. Assessments are not meant to give you some type of permanent label.

Don't make too much of where you fell statistically into this or that group, or how you compare with others. Just use it for a baseline of understanding who you are and to care for yourself and others. Your strengths are the unique colors on your palette. You have the opportunity to paint something in the world that no one else can. Tap into those colors and your unique way of expressing yourself.

When it comes to the world of sales, I really like CliftonStrengths for Sales.[14] It starts as a normal strength-finding test. That's interesting on its own, but then it evaluates you with respect to a selling role and gives you insight into how you can use these talents to succeed.

My top five themes are:

- Winning others over (Woo)—Spend time everyday interacting with people.

- Communication—Use your gift for stimulating conversation to connect with inspire others.

- Activator—Be a catalyst, when others are stuck make a decision and get going.

- Strategic—Always have at least three options in mind so you can adapt if circumstances change.

- Learner—Use your passion for learning to add value to your own and others' lives.

Most of my strengths are related to influencing and strategic thinking. I'm the idea fountain who can get a group inspired and moving, but execution and making things happen don't come as naturally to me. I need to partner with other individuals who have those strengths so that it's greater than what I could do on my own.

If we're not careful, our strengths can get in the way of our success when it comes to sales. For example, these are my top five themes through the lens of being aware of their dangers.

- Woo—Your sales conversations might focus more on socializing than on getting the sale or avoiding uncomfortable conversations.

- Communication—You tend to talk more than listen, or you might try to fill an uncomfortable silence during negotiation with customers who prefer to process, think, and review without commentary.

- Activator—Prospects may see your impulse to move quickly as unnecessary pressure.

- Strategic—Your quick, agile thinking might overwhelm a customer who wants a specific answer to a specific question. They also might find your creative and holistic strategy hard to accept.

- Learner—Your desire to constantly learn might keep you from feeling like you know enough.

It's easy to get lost in the sea of personal assessments. Instead, I encourage you to act on what you learn about yourself. Anytime you take an assessment, make a note of your strengths and describe how each one contributes or detracts from your success. This self-awareness is crucial because it helps you avoid the pitfalls of operating out of your weakness.

The art you create will always have a bigger impact if it maximizes your natural gifts. As author and mythologist, Joseph Campbell called it, "Follow your bliss."

But this isn't just about you. It's also about your team, if you're a leader or owner. This isn't a book on how to be a Business Artist just like me. Rather, it is for you to discover how to be one yourself and lead others in helping them identify their artistic style.

They say that people don't leave a company, they leave a manager. It's not true. People leave companies all the time because their gifts are not maximized. People go where they are appreciated, valued, and wanted.

However, it's hard to feel valued for who you are if you don't know who you are to begin with. While assessments can help you learn about yourself, sometimes you have to look past the data and listen to your instincts in order to innovate.

Innovate by Ignoring the Data

Earlier in the book, I talked about the problem of *dataism*—the tendency for modern culture, particularly business, to be based on data. We tend to approach data as if it's infallible, almost like some sort of higher being that's guiding us.

We should never blindly accept someone's interpretation of data. Anyone who's ever taken a statistics course knows the danger of trusting data, stats, surveys, or other ways of collecting and analyzing information. Who is doing the asking? How is information gathered? Why is it being gathered in the first place? All those are valid questions we should not ignore.

All that aside, though, let me pose the question of how we should interpret data and when we should follow it.

I recently read the book *Invent and Wander: The Collected Writings of Jeff Bezos.*[15] Bezos is a great example of a Business Artist when it comes to disruption and innovation. The book recounts a fascinating aspect of Amazon's journey. If Bezos had always listened to the data, he probably never would have started Amazon or led many of the innovations that we now accept as a standard part of Amazon.

Take the launch of Amazon Prime, for example. It began when one of his board members suggested that Amazon have a loyalty program similar to airlines with frequent flyer miles. Separately, an Amazon engineer suggested they offer free shipping to its most loyal customers. Bezos put these ideas together and requested that his team figure out if it would be worth it. The answer was a resounding no, at least from a profit perspective.

However, Bezos had a rule to use his heart and intuition in addition to empirical data in making decisions. He knew that creating Amazon Prime was a one-way door. It would be a difficult decision to reverse. Once people had access to free shipping and other features that might be included in Prime, they wouldn't want to give them up.

While Amazon was unprofitable with Prime in the beginning, it led to a combination of more loyalty and convenience, as well as a huge source of customer data. (I find it ironic that although in this instance Bezos didn't act according to data, Amazon uses data on its customers to keep them coming back and being loyal.)

Historian Walter Isaacson wrote the introduction to *Invent and Wander.* He claimed that while many people are smart, that's not what makes them special. Smart people are a dime a dozen and often don't find success. Isaacson reflects on figures like Leonardo da Vinci, Ben Franklin, Steve Jobs, and Albert Einstein. Each one was not only smart, but imaginative. That's what makes someone a true innovator.

Imagination is a byproduct of creative thinking, which, of course, begins in the mind. That's why caring for your cognition (your thinking processes) is such a critical element of mental health.

Caring for your Cognition

Have you ever had your computer freeze up while having too many applications open? This happens when you have exceeded the available random-access memory (RAM). Human brains are no different. The only difference is that you can't easily upgrade your brain to include more RAM like you can with computers.

Why does this matter to a Business Artist?

Just like the RAM in your computer, your brain has a finite amount of cognitive capacity each day. That's why you must pay attention to how much brain energy you're using. Creative thinking and creative tasks require massive amounts of capacity, which is why we sometimes procrastinate and avoid them.

If your brain was a computer, the Business Artist would be the memory-hogging application. It takes a lot of capacity to bring your art to life. On the other hand, consumption requires minimal capacity, so we do that by default, especially if we have mismanaged our finite resources.

How many times have you heard someone say (or perhaps you've said it yourself), "I was going to try it a new way this time, but I don't have the energy." This begs the question, "Why do we often feel we don't have the energy?"

For starters, just like a computer, we have too many mental applications running in the background. Think about all the cognitive applications you have going on right now while you're reading this book. You're probably fighting to pay attention because you have a dozen things to get done, and can't do them all at once.

As Gloria Mark, a writer for *Time* magazine, suggests in her article "Doing Nothing," a lack of activity can actually make you more productive. She writes, "When we are tired, our resistance to distractions declines, and it's not just external distractions, like notifications or targeted ads, that lead our attention astray. In fact, we found that we are just as likely to interrupt ourselves, thinking of something unrelated to the task at hand while trying to focus."[16]

We live in a society where success is judged by productivity and output. It's never been so easy to be tempted by the illusion that if you get through your inbox quickly, rapidly respond to Slack messages, overly schedule your day with Zoom calls, post and comments on LinkedIn and other social media sites, you believe you were somewhat productive. We spend a lot of time on unproductive work, but we feel good about it because we have kept busy and checked a lot of tasks off our to-do list.

How often do we stop and ask ourselves whether those tasks should have been done in the first place? How often do we lead our lives with intention and purpose? One of the easiest ways to do this is by paying attention to our sleep.

Sleep and Cognition

Sleep is a hot topic. Few people are getting enough of it, and we've also started to see the true connection between sleep and many aspects of our creativity and productivity.

When it comes to sleep, we categorize people into early birds and night owls. Early birds do their most productive work in the morning, and night owls do their most productive work at night. Studies suggest that early birds are more effective and intelligent compared to night owls. But as we get older, this correlation is less prominent.

Conventional wisdom says the early bird gets the worm, but the truth is that the worm can be eaten at any hour. We all have different biological rhythms and chronotypes. Figuring out when you are biologically *in the zone* can be transformational.

The main point I want to make is that sleep can supercharge your learning and development as a creative thinker. Sleeping after learning is like hitting the *save* button on work to make sure new memories aren't forgotten. This is when the vulnerable short-term memory bank does a file transfer to long-term storage through electronic activity that you can see when deep sleep brain waves are recorded.

In addition, Matt Walker's TED talk called "Sleep Is Your Superpower" shows new research demonstrating how you need sleep not just after but also before learning in order to prepare your brain. In one study, researchers took a group that had a full night's sleep and a group that had no sleep overnight, put them through an MRI, and gave them a list of things to remember. The group without sleep had a 40 percent deficit.[17]

If you're going to care for yourself as a creator, it doesn't necessarily mean making all kinds of radical changes in your life today. It might just mean getting a better night's sleep.

It's just not about the sleep itself. It's what it can do for you physically, emotionally, and cognitively. As you'll read in the next chapter, when you're at your best, you're able to bring that energy and creative thinking into collaborations where you can accomplish far more than you ever could on your own.

12

ENGAGING WITH COLLABORATORS

If you had to choose an animal that best represents the image of a stereotypical entrepreneur, which one would it be?

Would you choose an *eagle* that has incredible vision? How about an *elephant* that has great long-term memory and high emotional intelligence? Maybe a *dog* that is loyal and loves to play? Or maybe an *octopus* that has eight arms so it can multitask?

Those are all great possibilities, but the animal that best represents the traditional image of an entrepreneur is a *lone wolf.* Business literature over the last few decades is filled with stories about visionary founders who singlehandedly built a company through sheer grit and determination. But those stories are mostly myths.

Take Elon Musk, for example. While he's a brilliant innovator, the lore surrounding him promotes a cult of personality that feeds the perception that he alone charted the success of Tesla and SpaceX.

The reality is far more nuanced. J. B. Straubel was the unheralded technical expert behind Tesla's pioneering battery designs. Gwynne Shotwell provided vital leadership to turn SpaceX into a commercial space giant. And behind both stand thousands of engineers, designers, and employees who brought the ideas to life.

When you see a towering achievement in technology, business, or the arts, it may seem like the result of one brilliant mind. Michelangelo was the visionary and designer of the Sistine Chapel, yet had many artists working under him. Any great achievement is the result of lots of people working together.

In the previous chapter, we focused on some ways you can bring out your best as a creator and artist. In this chapter, we'll expand our focus to think about some ways to move beyond autonomy and begin to collaborate more effectively with teams, partners, direct reports, supervisors, and your closest clients or customers.

Challenging Collective Illusions

Let's begin with a concept you may not have heard before, but I promise is an integral concept related to collaboration: collective illusions. Here's a short summary based on work from Todd Rose, the author of the book *Collective Illusions*, as well as a YouTuber on one of my favorite channels, Big Think.[18]

Collective illusions refers to a situation where most people in a group go along with an opinion they don't agree with because they incorrectly believe that the majority agrees with it. In other words, the majority thinks most of the others in the group believe something they don't actually believe.

We've known about the phenomenon of *collective illusions* for over a hundred years, but our cultural and technological conditions have changed. Today, creating and sustaining these illusions is so easy that they flourish at a speed we've never seen in history. Technology has made it easy to sustain collective illusions on how to love, live, dress, and treat each other.

The Business Artist has the ability, and the responsibility, to challenge collective illusions in their workplaces and their lives. As we shine a light on these collective illusions on trust, success, and social norms, we have to ask ourselves, *What have we become?*

One of the biggest collective illusions is defining what a successful life is. Most of us believe the same illusion the majority believes, that fame, wealth, and status are what constitute success. But in private research from Big Think, Todd Rose asserted that most people in private believe that success is more due to personal fulfillment than work achievements. However, the private beliefs get hidden away in favor of what most people espouse publicly, even though that's not really what they believe. Those external perceptions get passed down through generations as a social norm, so the next generation believes what we perceive today's majority believes, even if it's inaccurate.[19]

Where did this illusion that we only exist for personal fulfillment come from? It began in the workplace.

The Importance of Trust

In Chapter 1, I mentioned Frederick Taylor, who wrote *The Principles of Scientific Management*, which focused on his ideas for creating a productive economy. He believed we weren't very efficient in our business practices and that one of the first things you need to do is stop trusting people.

Taylor invented a top-down systems approach governed by managers. He is credited with inventing the word *manager* and saw workers simply as *cogs* who operated in a system far more important than any individual worker.

Because of how our institutions treat us by removing choices and assuming we are not trustworthy, Todd Rose argues that we have come to see each other that way. We assume most people can't be trusted, so we are always suspicious of others.

This reminds me of a chat I had with a sales leader at one of the largest network security businesses in the world. We were discussing the role of the Business Artist, and he said, "Adam, I get what you are saying. Maybe for some, that kind of thinking and approach would be helpful to them and their business, but we can't trust everyone, you know? We need to grow 30 percent this year, which we can only do if people follow the process we've put in front of them and don't veer too much from this. I don't want our sales guys going around trying new experiments and innovating. It may not work, and it doesn't scale."

I actually agree with parts of what he said. To be clear, being a Business Artist is not about undertaking risky experiments all day long. It's more like an 80/20 rule where 20 percent of the time you are living out your art at work, and the other 80 percent you are focused on the processes or tasks assigned to you. But the bottom line is that managers and leaders must trust our teams to find the right balance for them and our business.

Having trust allows us to freely collaborate with others. Successful collaboration is about being vulnerable and giving up more in the beginning. When you collaborate with contractors and people outside your workplace, for example, you also gain access to their network. This is true in the traditional arts and in business as well. You can't underestimate the power of networking and community building.

We can have collective illusions on any topic you can imagine. For example, when it comes to the topic of success, most would rate *fame* as an element of success that others would prioritize. However, when people give their private opinions, it scores dead last when it comes to priorities. We don't care about fame, but we believe most people do. Success is ultimately whatever you make of it.

Another example: when it comes to social and cultural norms, these are most often the ones that are challenged by artists. This is why you see movements led by artists but not by the business itself. No one at the record company is coming up with new music ideas and movements. The artists are the ones who help our society progress, not just in art, but also in social norms. Art is never isolated by itself because it's always attached to other types of social progress.

By this point in the book, I hope you are convinced that collaboration is an excellent goal for your creative life and your business. But collaboration is not just a *nice-to-have* aspect of creativity. It's essential to the creative process—so much so that things can get a little dangerous when collaboration is absent.

Moving Past the Lone Wolf Mentality

All this points to the need for artists to not only focus on developing their craft, but also on the skill of human relationships. To put it in mathematical terms, collaboration is not like algebra, which focuses on operations. It's more like geometry, which focuses on angles and shapes. It's also like calculus, which focuses on change.

Why are so many artists scared to collaborate? How do we get past the lone wolf mentality that so many creative people struggle with?

Some artists feel the power of their work will be watered down if they bring in other people. They are afraid of compromising their artistic vision, losing creative control, or feeling stripped of the validation that comes from finishing something.

For example, why would an author not want to publicly credit a ghostwriter? Maybe the author is afraid it will destroy the perception that they are a real expert or authority. In recent years, it's been refreshing to see a reversal of this trend. Many authors who use ghostwriters are quick to give their collaborators credit. It's not only a more honest representation of who created the book. It also says to the world that the author made a wise choice to stick to their zone of genius and hire a professional writer to do the heavy lifting of the book.

This is usually the case when you look at successful artists in any field. They not only collaborate often, but they also give credit to their collaborators. Even when you think someone did it all themselves (or they say they did), I can assure you they probably had help, inspiration, and input from others, whether they were credited or not.

Maybe it helps to look at collaboration in a different way. It can be helpful to reframe the idea of collaboration to strengthen and enhance creative vision and voice rather than as a threat to artistic identity.

This often happened when I worked in consulting. For example, I assigned a piece of creative work for a sales proposal to a colleague. They said, "Cool, I'll have it to you by Monday." Monday rolled around, and nothing. At the end of the day, I asked to see where they were. They said they needed more time and that it would be great. Then Tuesday came, and there was another delay. At that point, I said, "Just send what you've got. I'd love to help."

Finally, Wednesday came around. My colleague had worked on several versions of it independently, and the work product was creative, but I still had some feedback to offer. However, it was getting late, and we needed to get it to the client. The colleague had so much individual ownership of their output that they were unconsciously defensive to any critique.

I've also been on the other side of this many times. You feel like each time you ask for more time, whatever you are creating has to be improved. When you finally deliver it, you are expecting praise and validation, and it's hard to accept any criticism. You end up feeling defeated and a bit ashamed of yourself for the long delay.

Instead, if you had taken the chance to collaborate at the beginning, welcome critique on early drafts, and continued to improve, you would have had a better output and felt more fulfillment from the creative process.

The story above presents an excellent example of the "Ikea Effect." Ikea, the furniture retailer, is known for selling products you have to assemble yourself. The Ikea Effect is a cognitive bias where we place a disproportionately high value on products or projects we have created or invested effort into building.

People feel a sense of pride, ownership, and accomplishment when they have put effort into building something, even if it is not objectively superior to a comparable product they bought off the shelf or that someone else created. This bias can lead people to overvalue their own creations and invest more effort than necessary to complete a project.

Why are we artists wired this way in the first place? What about our creative wiring keeps us from great collaborative partnerships? Let's look at a few reasons.

Five Habits That Kill Collaboration

I don't know if I'd say there are personality traits that specifically prevent collaboration. Great artists can have any personality style. Many of history's greatest creative minds were known for being prickly, moody, or even downright cruel at times. But that doesn't mean it's okay to push people away.

I would argue that their "anti-people" approach probably worked against them. They succeeded *in spite* of being difficult or prickly.

How can you and I avoid the same creative and emotional landmines that prevent great collaboration? Here are five common habits that destroy great partnerships:

1. **Obsession with perfectionism:** Artists who are too attached to achieving a particular vision or aesthetic may resist input from others. Obviously, this makes it hard to meaningfully collaborate because it makes the relationship difficult.

2. **Attachment to ego:** Artists focused on establishing their own brand or reputation may be hesitant to share the spotlight or credit with others. This can create conflicts and tension in collaborative settings.

3. **Unwillingness to compromise:** If you're working with a partner but cannot find common ground, the collaboration will be strained. The best creative partnerships always have some give and take.

4. **Failure to communicate:** Communication is key to collaboration, and collaboration is key to business artistry.

Artists who struggle to communicate effectively, whether due to shyness, social anxiety, or language barriers, may have difficulty building relationships with potential collaborators.

5. **Inability to trust:** Artists who have had negative experiences with collaboration in the past, such as being overruled or marginalized by other collaborators, may be hesitant to collaborate in the future. Without trust, creating a space where artists can collaborate is impossible.

No Business Artist is perfect. We all have continual inner work to avoid these five negative habits. If you're in a leadership role, how can you create a setting where these habits are minimized and healthy partnerships can blossom?

Creating Collaborate Environments

To do this, leaders may need to shift to or promote a leadership style that emphasizes openness, empathy, and inclusivity. I know these are all buzzwords today, but collaboration cannot happen without them. It's not just one leader's job, though. An organization needs to have a culture that values and supports creative people.

It's hard for innovation to happen in an environment where people don't work together, work in silos, and refuse to collaborate.

Easier said than done, right? I've seen many companies that want to create a culture of innovation which encourages collaboration and risk-taking. However, they can also struggle to get there since they don't have solid foundational principles in place. We've taken individuals through innovation workshops where they come up with amazing new ideas only to be disappointed when the culture swallows up their creativity later on.

We saw this with Walt Disney Animation Studios. After Roy Disney helped push Michael Eisner out of the CEO job at Disney, Bob Iger replaced him and was eager to get the company back on track.

One of his first moves was a bid to buy Pixar for over $7 billion and give them control to help fix their creative culture problem.

After releasing several hand-drawn animation hits such as *The Lion King*, *Aladdin*, and *The Little Mermaid*, they were struggling with flop after flop and needed to pivot from a culture that had been sucking the life out of the artistry. Iger saw buying Pixar as the only way forward, and it has become one of the most successful media partnerships of all time.

You don't have to be Disney to experience the amazing power of collaboration. Anyone can harness its power, no matter what your area of creative work or the size of your company or team (or even if you're a solopreneur).

Here are a few important strategies to keep in mind as you pursue more collaboration:

1. **Build trust through communication and modeling.** It's important to be transparent and consistent in your communication and model the behavior you expect from others. This helps create a culture of openness and accountability. Innovation can occur when Business Artists can freely express their ideas and offer critique even to their supervisors

2. **Encourage diverse perspectives:** Related to building trust, leaders can encourage collaboration by actively seeking out and valuing diverse perspectives and experiences. They can also create opportunities for individuals to share their ideas and feedback in a safe and respectful environment. This allows for creative iteration without judgment.

3. **Stay open-minded:** Leaders of Business Artists need to be open to new ideas and approaches. They must also be willing to consider different perspectives. As a result, they are more likely to be able to work collaboratively with others.

4. **Be flexible:** Leaders should be able to provide flexibility and see that the way they work may not be the only way to operate. They need to give freedom and responsibility to the Business Artists in their organization to thrive. This means letting go of individualistic tendencies, guided by a balance of structure and unstructured space.

5. **Recognize and celebrate success:** Too often, I see only the sellers praised. Leaders should celebrate the team, both individually and collectively, as often as possible. Bring new creative approaches and innovations forward with praise, not just by communicating sales numbers. Recognize the good collaboration it took to get it done. It will help build a culture of collaboration and continuous improvement.

A final thought on the importance of recognition: We've talked in earlier chapters about the disease of output, which is the tendency to measure your value by your output. This temptation is felt particularly by younger workers, and as a result, they focus on quantity over quality. They develop a lot of anxiety because they think they need to be a rapid responder to any text, email, or Slack message.

I think COVID exacerbated this a bit. Sometimes, we find ourselves optimizing output, speed, and productivity at the expense of good collaboration and creativity. We need to continuously celebrate creativity if we want our organizations and businesses to grow.

Now that we've spent some time considering how to care for ourselves as creators and engage with others in collaboration, let's turn our attention to how we can make a bigger difference in our companies.

13

ADDING VALUE
TO YOUR COMPANY

If you spend much time in entrepreneurial circles, you'll likely hear someone say a version of the phrase, "Remember that people are always tuned in to WIIFM: What's In It For Me?"

It's a great reminder that your customers and clients are mostly concerned about how your products and services can help them. It might be their health, wealth, relationships, productivity, status, or any of a thousand needs we have as humans. They want a tangible result in exchange for the money they are paying.

It's not just customers and clients who are tuned into WIIFM. Anyone who works for a company is listening to the same station. When we're working for someone else, we want to know how the work benefits us. Think of all the job interviews you've sat in during your career. The first thing on your mind is not how you can help the company. Instead, you're thinking about the salary, benefits, vacation time, work environment, job perks, or how this role will help you learn and grow.

That's all well and good! Any intelligent person would consider those things. Yet, at the same time, you need to think about the broader picture. Your work at the company or organization is not just about you.

As the poet John Donne once wrote, "No man is an island." We began Part 3 of this book with the concept of concentric circles. You, as the artist, are in the center because your work as a Business Artist begins with you, your dreams and goals, your health and wellness, and your passion and energy. But it can't stay there.

As we moved outward, we talked about how to engage with collaborators and build excellent working relationships. After all, if you're not healthy and focused as an artist, that *unwellness* will spread to your relationships, partnerships, and collaborations. If you're going to operate in *harmony*, it has to extend to your relationships. No Business Artist relationship is more important than the one you have with collaborators.

But it doesn't stop there. In this chapter, we move to the third level of concentric circles as we focus on how you can add value to your company. This is a complex topic! The phrase "adding value" is pretty vague, and we could write a whole book on just this concept alone. Many people have! I don't need to duplicate their insights here.

Instead, I want to share my perspective and some practical advice and tools on how to not just be a *team player* for your company, but how to be essential. Let's begin by laying the groundwork of what it means to be in business in the first place, particularly in the world of sales.

Keeping Two Buyers in Mind

A sales interaction is like a jazz ensemble. The sellers and customers or clients are all playing the same song, but each one is improvising. No two performances are ever exactly the same.

One of the most important instruments in the sales ensemble is the customer. In a subscription-based world, they become the lead instrument. If they don't buy because the band couldn't keep up or follow where they wanted to go, that's where you get churn.

That's why we must remember that we can't just focus on the buyer of the product or service. You need to be aware of the customers you aren't talking to—the tinkerers, the explorers—the ones who might even be your initial entry into the business to begin with. Don't forget about them because they can be key players in this whole business equation.

For example, at Meahana, the actual business buyer of our collaboration software is often different from the actual end users who will create and facilitate on our platform.

As sellers, we were taught in generic sales books that in our accounts, "We need to get our teams to go higher and wider." In some cases and industries, that might still be true. But more and more end users are doing their own *trial purchases* internally, testing new tools and products, building an internal community and coalition of other users, and making changes from within. The purpose of all this effort is to lead to a purchase and have a stake in the successful adoption.

Today, we often call these individuals the "champions," but that can sometimes just be your fan or deal coach. What you really need to find are the end users who have social power or influence. We all know who these people are in our companies. A simple way to discover them is to redraw the corporate organizational chart, remove all the titles, and just build it for who has the most *followers* or sphere of influence.

That would be pretty useful knowledge for a seller trying to find the person with a lot of social power who can have the biggest influence on whether your solution is adopted. They will have *skin in the game* and be more open to a successful adoption.

Keep in mind, though, that not all companies are the same. Business Artists can show up in every type and size of company. Knowing the growth models of major types of companies can help you better understand how to engage with them, their potential concerns, and the kind of dynamics they (and you) might be dealing with.

Three Types of Growth Models

You can segment companies in many different ways: by industry, size, philosophy, and probably even political aspiration in some cases. But I've found the following way of thinking about companies to be quite useful over my sales career. Each one has a different approach to creative problem-solving for customers.

1. **Product-Led Growth Companies**

   A dead giveaway for these companies is that they feature a *Try Now* button all over their website. The main goal is simply to get the sale. This sort of bottom-up sales approach is already happening in product-led growth companies. These are the ones where you go to their websites, see what they sell and what the pricing options are, perhaps try it for free for a limited time, or even purchase without talking to a single seller.

   It may be a *show, don't tell* philosophy to help customers start their purchase journey with a real understanding of what they are committing to. Many companies are moving in this direction, and this is a new role for the Business Artist seller.

   For example, you might find a customer with high trial usage and reach out to see if they'd like to upgrade to some additional features for a payment today. By contrast, it's a different conversation when you're talking to someone already using your product or service. Business Artist buyers love these types of companies as they give them an easy way to try the product.

2. **Sales-Led Growth Companies**

   In contrast to product-led companies, sales-led growth companies have *Contact Us* buttons all over their website. When you go to their website, it's hard sometimes to tell what they actually do, what they sell, or how much it costs.

Consulting companies and large enterprise business-to-business (B2B) companies fit here. They offer mostly points of view (POVs), thought leadership documents, case studies, and related types of content.

Even if they have a product page, you'll be met with a *Contact Us* button. Business Artists thrive in these types of companies. Why? Because it's more about relationships and human connections, and the possibilities those open up versus a person coming in already knowing what they want. Instead, they get to self-discover and potentially co-create with others.

3. **Marketing-Led Growth Company**

    This type of company is rarer than the first two, although it's important in e-commerce and film and entertainment. When it comes to companies that are led by marketing growth, there are precise formulas that calculate how much advertising money and endless other factors it takes to generate sales. If you take away their creative marketing, they are just another product in a crowded market.

    Sellers at product-led growth companies tend to be more junior, more data-driven in their approach, and task-focused. ("I can see you're using X number of services already, sir.") The product is the most powerful piece of the company vehicle, as opposed to a sales-led company where the sellers get all the glory and praise inside the company.

    Now that we've established some groundwork for how to think about the context of a company and what type of company you work for, we'll spend the rest of this chapter looking at some tools and techniques for improving your daily and weekly routines. Don't look at this as a checklist or a collection of items to try all at once. These are just tools that can help you in a variety of ways. I encourage you to choose a couple of them right now, put them into practice, and then try and work the rest into your routine over time.

When you practice these, it not only adds value to you as a Business Artist. It also enhances your colleagues, collaborators, and, ultimately, the company.

Use Limiting Constraints

Sometimes, we think of creativity as a force that requires no limits. We use phrases like "out of the box thinking" to describe what the creative process should feel like. However, limits are not just helpful. They are essential. In the real world, creativity has limits. There's no such thing as unlimited time, money, personnel, or resources. This is why limiting constraints can be so helpful to the work of Business Artists.

My sister, Lindsay, is an elementary school teacher. She reminded me that limiting constraints can be essential for learning and development. At recess, she gives her third-grade students three objects to play with. There are only three, and they are generally new objects.

I asked her what typically happens in this situation. She said that at first, they look bored but quickly get *unstuck* and figure out new games and ways to use these objects. After they have exhausted all possibilities, she gives them three new objects.

When you limit your constraints and *put yourself in a box*, it probably feels like you're leaving out key elements of the task or compromising yourself somehow. But remember that constraints breed creativity. Look at this from the perspective of music. Once you play a note, you are already bound to what will sound good next to it. You have to start somewhere.

One powerful question to help with problem-solving is asking, "To what end?" These three words are a powerful force when innovating because they keep the larger purpose in mind.

Have you ever been asked to "blue sky" a solution or idea? It means that you assume there aren't any constraints—literally, the *sky* is the limit (with a blue sky indicating that conditions are perfect because there isn't a cloud in the sky).

If you *blue sky* a solution, the biggest challenge you face is: where to start? It feels like the intimidating blinking cursor on a new document. Starting with a blank slate is not only challenging in the space of innovation, but it's also not efficient.

At Meahana, we encourage the use of templates in workplaces as a way to save time, but they're only a starting point. A template that can't be customized is not art of any kind. Rather, it is a repetition exercise, a print reproduction that lacks free expression and ownership.

It's easy to bend your knee to the power of conformity in a business setting. The group tends to get annoyed with that person, or two, who always sees things differently and can cut through the noise. That person generally has done a lot of work in creative constraints and is an expert at convergent thinking. Treasure these people because it's very hard to innovate without them.

Connecting the Dots

In 1962, Sarnoff Mednick began studying creative cognition, which is to say the cognitive process underlying creative performance. In the study, Mednick was able to link creativity to associative thinking. In the test, they gave groups words to associate. This list comprised pairs of indirectly related (for example, "cat" and "cheese") and unrelated word pairs (for example, "subject" and "marriage").

Compared to the less creative group, the more creative group reported smaller distances between words that were unrelated. This can be interpreted as finding creative associations between words that are not usually related to each other.[20]

As your brain is able to find smaller distances between things, you'll be able to quickly translate thoughts and ideas from one discipline to another. You can connect the dots on *how selling can be like jazz* or any number of metaphors that will help you communicate to customers more effectively and at a human level.

Being a generalist triumphs over-specialization. Over time, and especially now that the world is becoming more and more complex, the world needs generalists who can connect the dots across a number of different topics and domains of expertise.

This is especially important when bringing art and creative thinking into your company. Why? Because your company needs team members who can innovate by putting together ideas, subjects, or concepts they haven't connected before. This is the very nature of creativity.

Try this exercise. Ask someone to explain their favorite hobby and why they love it. Then ask, "How is doing your job like this?" For example, my hobby is to play piano and occasionally produce music. My job as the CEO of a software startup is like making music because I have to take inspiration externally from my customers or the world. I also have to experiment with new ideas to create something new to solve a challenge.

Here's another example. Let's say your hobby is photography, and you're a software engineer. You could say that your job as an engineer is like photography because there is no single way to get the right shot, just like in writing code. There is repetition, trial and error, and surprisingly, lots of math involved in how you do it.

To close out this chapter, I want to zoom out a little bit and look at the bigger picture of how to add value to your company or organization. You have to do all the things we've talked about in this chapter to have a proper perspective of sales and enhance your creative thinking. But if you're not optimizing your mental and physical energy, you'll always be fighting against yourself.

It's especially important if you run a small business or are a solopreneur. You're shouldering more of the load than you would if you're an employee in a big company. But regardless of your role, it's essential to take care of yourself. One of the best ways to do that is through the power of meditation.

The Power of Meditation

I'm thankful that we have begun to awaken to the value of self-care in the business community. Yes, we must move products, engage in sales, and do all the things associated with creating profit. But we're not soulless robots. We are humans whose energy needs replenishing every day.

One of the ways we can do this is through meditation. People approach meditation in many different ways. I see meditation as witnessing your inner thinking and removing its pattern-driven behavior. I'm somewhat new to meditation, but I find it to be a mind and body hack to reset, recharge, and get myself unstuck.

There are many types of meditation, but nine of them are broadly accepted and can be useful for the Business Artist:

1. Mindfulness meditation

2. Spiritual meditation

3. Focused meditation

4. Movement meditation

5. Mantra meditation

6. Transcendental meditation

7. Progressive relaxation

8. Loving-kindness meditation

9. Visualization meditation

The most popular and easiest to do alone is *mindfulness meditation*. This refers to the practice of noticing your thoughts without judging or interacting with them. It takes practice, but it clears out the mental debris, giving you a renewed *blank slate* feeling to try a new approach or idea. My second favorite is *focused meditation*, in which you use your senses to concentrate. Moon gazing or staring at a burning candle are good examples of focused meditation. As the name suggests, this practice is ideal for anyone who wants to sharpen their focus and attention.

Even if you are not doing one of the major forms of meditation, simply breathing with your eyes closed is the quickest way to change your perspective. It sounds counter-intuitive, but there is a lot of productivity embedded in stillness. When you take ten minutes to reflect with your eyes closed, you will find new creative paths you missed and value how your time is spent next.

If you listen to a symphony, there are movements where the music changes or a good DJ set where there are long, slower, trance-like breaks for us as an audience to catch our breath from the dancing and reflect. One of my favorite tracks to reflect on is *Polaris* by Deadmau5. It starts off calm, celestial, and inward. It will make the noise in your brain disappear and go to other places. The song then jumps into a dance beat where you can choose to open your eyes again, move around, and get ready for your next task with a new perspective.

Another favorite of mine is *Primavera* by Ludovico Einaudi. Primavera means "Spring" in Italian. If you go in with that mental image, imagine while listening that you are a small flower seed planted into the earth. As you rise to the surface through the soil, your journey begins soft and gentle, then beating rains push you back and forth. As it calms, you push higher, almost blooming, before getting beaten down again. Enriched by the rain, you rise stronger toward the sun.

For others, the song may not resemble this, but that is not the point. Instead, the main idea of meditating with music is to give it a mental narrative, something to focus on, a story that will transport you on a journey.

Smiling also brings energy into the world. It's a simple gift you can give to others. Try it at an airport—not on your way to the gate, but on the way off the plane through the terminal. There is so much stress on everyone's face that if you throw them off with a smile, it will be met with one in return. You've helped someone calm down or cheer up, and the validation you give yourself is free and fun.

I do this all the time at the airport. I look forward to it when I land to smile at approaching people on my way to exit. Give this a try—not only at the airport, but anytime you're around people. Let's face it: People are stressed and anxious everywhere they go!

One more suggestion related to meditation: Walking in the woods is great, especially if it is someplace you haven't been. My wife and I like to explore new hikes regularly everywhere we go. Many of my artistic ideas start with a reflection from nature. It will also give you calming serotonin and rewarding dopamine. Walking in the woods is a great stress relief, which is why so many people retreat to nature when they're feeling out of sorts.

As Business Artists, our role is to add value to customers and clients, our company, and our colleagues. We do this by keeping the end-user experience front of mind, understanding company dynamics, boosting creativity through new types of experiments, managing our energy, and bringing artistry into our daily work.

Ultimately, that sets us up for more success not just with our company but with the community at large. That's the topic of the next chapter.

14

CONTRIBUTING
TO THE COMMUNITY

What is the ultimate purpose of business? It's a philosophical question, to be sure, but an important one. We spend a pretty big chunk of our lives pouring into our careers. Shouldn't we have a clear idea of why we're doing all this in the first place?

We work to get a paycheck and make a living, of course. Without that, you just have an expensive hobby! But as we've talked about throughout this book, there is a great purpose to what we do as Business Artists. There's a broader meaning behind showing up to work each day and putting in the hours. It's not just about us as individuals or even our company. It's also about the difference we can make in our community.

We can define *community* in different ways. It can be the actual geographic location of your company, or it can be your industry or niche. It might even be the community of people who do the same kind of work you do across different industries or locations.

However you define your community, you can influence those outside of your company's direct sphere. You're ultimately more than an owner, worker, or employee. You're a Business Artist, a leader who can impact far more than the immediate context of your business.

The Business Artist's Responsibility

The very term "Business Artist" causes a little confusion sometimes. People generally think of business and art as two completely different realms of culture. One of the many differences that people perceive is how each area views the issue of "open vs. closed source." Let me explain.

Think about software for a moment. "Open source" refers to the idea that anyone should be able to use, change, or distribute the software. The key difference between open-source software and proprietary software is whether the source code is available.

In proprietary software, the source code isn't available to the public. Open-source software, however, is available for anyone to use however they want. This openness drives innovation and encourages contributions from a large community of developers, which leads to higher-quality software and a more secure and stable codebase.

Artists primarily operate from an *open-source* point of view. To be clear, I'm not talking about artistic plagiarism, but rather artistic inspiration. Artists have responsibilities to other artists. You don't see a lot of successful selfish artists as a result. It's quite the opposite.

Artists are quick to collaborate and be vulnerable. They are also quick to give up more in the beginning. We see this reflected in more collaboration of companies with partners and contracted employees. When you work this way, you also gain their entire network and get to *rent their perspective* rather than forcing them to come in and embrace your culture and way of thinking to be successful.

Bringing the conversation back to this chapter's topic, how do you grow a community? You start by aligning around a movement. That could be any social issue or way of living. You can do this by finding and promoting *positive deviants* in society. They are doing something different in private that violates a cultural norm.

I find it interesting that we typically use the word "deviant" to describe someone who is different in a negative way. To call someone a "deviant" is to accuse them of being the lowest version of a human they can be. By contrast, I'm advocating for us to be *positive deviants* in the sense that we are violating a cultural norm that perhaps shouldn't exist in the first place.

Here's one example. In the 1970s, Vietnam had a severe malnutrition problem. The government tried many top-down approaches to solve the issue. But as they were working on the problem, they discovered that healthy people also existed in the population, even in the poorest communities. They found the mothers of healthy kids were feeding them shrimp because it was widely available.

Somewhere in their history, there had been a cultural norm that made people believe that eating shrimp caused harm in some way. These moms were *positive deviants* because they'd found an unconventional way to solve the problem and shared it throughout their communities. So, the solution wasn't about telling the population what to eat, but rather to amplify the voices of these deviants to tell their stories. The new perspective about the nutrient-rich diet spread through the communities and solved the problem.

Being a *positive deviant* doesn't only mean focusing on huge, culture-wide problems. It can start right where you are in the smallest possible way, even with the next person you meet.

Remembering People's Names

One of the most basic things we can do to add value to others in our communities is simply to remember names. Sounds simple, right? But it's amazing how many people neglect this very basic human way of showing people they matter.

Remembering people's names is one of the biggest hacks the Business Artist can learn. When you develop this skill, it's useful for building relationships and for the broader application of memorizing and recalling information with ease.

Let's start with the basics by talking about encoding. Your brain is not a whiteboard. It is a complex neural network of electrons similar to a computer. Any information you send to a computer is encoded (and later decoded) for transmission and storage. When you hear information, an encoding process requires your full attention to form a strong memory trace.

If you are in a social setting or preoccupied with other thoughts, it's hard for that to happen. You'll get a weak encoding process, like when you get an MP3 that wasn't encoded properly and sounds terrible. You often have the added interference of trying to memorize another person's name before the first one was stored properly. We have a finite cognitive load, which refers to our working memory or attention capacity. When we are in a situation where we have to remember multiple names at once, the cognitive load increases quickly.

If you think of this like a computer, you have to first convert information to transmit and store it. You can only do this quickly and transfer a set number of new files at a time.

The trick is association. You need to be able to quickly offload new files from your working memory into a short-term folder that you can access. To do this, you need to efficiently find associations. Names are arbitrary labels that don't provide much context or connection to the person they represent. To remember a name effectively, it helps to associate it with other information, like a physical characteristic or someone else you know with that name.

I like to force myself to spell their name in my head or remember how they made me feel, what they remind me of, or a story I already know where I can put them in as a character. If their name is in a song I know or could make up, it helps quite a bit. It's easy to associate someone's name with information already in your brain until you can form a new memory link.

In my view, really good salespeople remember people's names and use them in their stories and communication. When I share this with people, I will inevitably get some form of pushback like, "I'm just bad at names."

I often respond like this: "Don't take this as me being offensive, but saying that you're bad at names just signals to me that you don't care. You don't care enough to keep your attention and focus when you meet people. When you check into a hotel, I'll bet you get your hotel key, go out to dinner later, go back to the hotel, and know right where to go. You cared enough to remember three to five new numbers and could store that information, make an association with it, and somehow remember it.

"If I asked you two days after you checked out, you wouldn't remember those numbers because you'd have no need to. We are capable of doing that with people's names as well. You can master it with the right practice if you want to dedicate attention to it."

When you remember a person's name, it will ensure they are more likely to remember yours. When I've been at conferences for two days and spent the effort to get names right at the beginning, it's fun to shake hands before leaving and say, "Great to meet you, Sarah, with an *h*, or Lindsay with an *a*."

They often say, "You as well. I'm so sorry, but can you remind me of your name?"

Give it a try. You'll feel incredible power in doing so! It's a small but powerful way to contribute to your community as a Business Artist.

Getting to Know Your Neighbors

Another powerful way to contribute is something you might not expect. In today's world, we're used to communicating with people all over the world. We live in a truly global village where business can be done with anyone who has an internet connection. Some entrepreneurs have embraced the "digital nomad life" where they're constantly on the road.

I say, "More power to them!" I'm grateful for the opportunities we have to live and do business any way we want. Yet at the same time, there's something to be said for the grounding that comes when we commit to a specific place. It's why Business Artists thrive in cities and diverse communities.

Research on the connection between urban density and creativity includes the work of Edward Glaeser, an economist known for his studies on urban economics. His book *Triumph of the City* is a valuable resource for understanding the relationship between urban density and innovation. In addition, Richard Florida, an urban theorist, has written extensively on the "creative class" and the role of cities in fostering creativity. His book *The Rise of the Creative Class* examines the importance of accessibility and connectivity in urban environments.

Getting to spend a lot of time in large urban cities around the world has fueled my belief that you need density, diversity, accessible transit, and good walkability to boost cognitive function and create collaborative communities organically. That is not to say you cannot be a Business Artist if you don't live in one of these areas.

There are already large amounts of creative individuals and an ecosystem that rewards and supports this type of work in these areas. These are some of the cities I have visited or worked in that have a lot of creative energy and great creative communities: San Francisco, New York, London, Berlin, Tokyo, Paris, Barcelona, and Amsterdam. I've also been told I need to get to Melbourne and Stockholm.

It might sound ironic, but even though I live in L.A., which is known as the entertainment capital of the world, I find it harder to engage creatively if you are just walking the streets and hoping for some spontaneous inspiration. If you are a Hollywood studio executive, you can drive from your gated house, out of your gated community, behind a tinted car window, to your gated studio lot, to your executive parking area, and into your executive elevator to your executive office. Nowhere in that whole sequence did you have to interact with anyone outside your socioeconomic sphere.

If you do this for a few years, it will change you. I've seen it up close and personal. Those people don't have the same spirit of openness, collaboration, and business creativity. Thankfully, the creatives around them and the ones they hire don't fall into this pattern, or we'd have some pretty lousy movies to watch and songs to listen to.

The creative community is very alive in L.A. for artists. However, I don't see the same for the big media companies, which is leading to a lot of disruption in their businesses.

Communities and collectives are important because they help reinforce artistic identity. For example, when you do CrossFit, you identify as a person who's part of that culture. "Oh yeah, I do CrossFit, bro!" The same is true for vegans. You'll know if you're talking to someone who does CrossFit or is a vegan because they wear that identity on their sleeve.

Identity matters. It's why I feel so passionate about the idea of being a Business Artist. It's my core identity. My colleagues at work would say this is true about me. Being a Business Artist is what I identify with and why I've written this book. People who also think of themselves as Business Artists will relate with me because we see the world the same way, even though we may come from different backgrounds. We inspire each other and the community where we live, whether at work or home.

Maybe the city you live in or the company where you work aren't known for creative ecosystems. You can still find or start a community. Find *your people*, the ones who will challenge and teach you, and those *you* can teach, and they'll do the same.

You can try to do this all on your own, but you'll go much further if you have the support of leadership in your organization or company.

The Leader's Role in Building Community

While this book is not just about changing the broader culture, it's hard to imagine a world where Business Artists thrive without strong leaders who value their creativity. Many CEOs, owners, and other leaders communicate some version of "we tolerate creativity" either explicitly or through their actions.

Setting the tone at the top, communicating the value of creativity, and demonstrating openness to new ideas is paramount. Leaders who promote a growth mindset in their communities must emphasize the value of learning and embracing challenges. This mindset can help employees feel more comfortable taking risks and proposing creative solutions.

Here are a few concrete suggestions for leaders:

- **Ask often, "What can we learn from this?"** This question helps you reflect on situations that might not have gone well but gave you the opportunity to learn from failure. Success isn't always the best teacher because you don't know what to correct for next time.

- **Implement reward and recognition programs.** These programs should acknowledge and celebrate creative efforts, even if they don't show immediate results. People will repeat behavior that is rewarded.

- **Organize events to bring people together.** This can include cross-functional workshops, team-building exercises, or innovation challenges to bring people together from different backgrounds.

- **Make time for innovation.** Allocate time for creativity, but be careful with this as you grow. Google used to have an 80/20 rule where employees could spend 20 percent of their time on creativity. However, as the company grew, they needed more focus, which resulted in more tightly targeted innovation activities.

- **Start the learning process.** Provide resources and training programs that help employees build their creative skills and learn about innovation strategies. The ones that really get into it will start to learn on their own and teach others.

- **Add creativity to your dashboard.** Monitor the progress and success of creative initiatives so that they demonstrate their value to the organization. Make sure everyone has access to this information so they can see real-time progress updates.

As someone who has spent over a decade on the people side of strategy execution, I've seen countless cultural shifts where companies have transformed their image from being non-innovative to becoming leaders in creativity. The same is true in the opposite direction. For every Kodak, Blackberry, Yahoo, and Blockbuster, there is a re-invented Microsoft, LEGO, IBM, or Adobe.

Dealing with Division

As we consider ways to add value to our communities, it might be worth pausing to ask an important question. With so much social and political division today, how does it affect our efforts to be good citizens and Business Artists? Or is some of this *division* simply a mirage we can ignore?

I don't believe the world is as divided as we think. This goes back to the concept of collective illusions. The media (including social media) has made us believe that division is far more extreme than it actually is. When you sit down and talk to people who are different than you, you can easily find common ground.

Divisions or differences between people, such as those based on race, gender, or political beliefs, have been exaggerated or reinforced by social and cultural factors. These divisions are not inherent. They have been created through narratives we have passed down and continue to perpetuate.

Media of every kind contributes to this sense of division and polarization by emphasizing differences and stoking fear, even when these differences may be superficial. Nobody wants to read an article about unity and working together because we have a deep tendency to huddle together in our tribes.

The job of TV networks and social media apps is to keep eyeballs on their products so they can pay advertisers. Therefore, it's in their best interests to keep people hyped up and relying on them to reinforce their perspective on a perceived enemy.

You cannot be an effective Business Artist if you only receive input from people who think, act, or look like you. We need to have more friendly discourse in our society. We also need to remember the principles of a good argument. It starts with acknowledging the other point of view, restating it in your own words, asking for agreement, and then offering your counterpoint.

Artists accept and give criticism all the time. It doesn't have to mean we are divided. We just have to be smart about how we accept and receive criticism. A good dose of humility and empathy never hurt anyone.

The Importance of Empathy

One of the running themes of this book is the importance of empathy. It means the ability to not only understand the feelings of another person, but also feel them on some level. It doesn't mean you have to agree, but it does mean you appreciate and respect their point of view and experience.

Unfortunately, in today's business culture, empathy is often seen as a weakness, particularly by Type-A business leaders who are hard-driving and just want to run over everyone else. How can we lose the stigma that empathy equals weakness?

We have long-held cultural norms in many companies, regions, and within pop culture that need to be challenged for this stigma to vanish. We can start by having more TV shows like *Ted Lasso*. It's a great reminder that shows don't have to involve us rooting for some megalomaniac tyrant (see *House of Cards, Billions*, or *Succession*). While those shows may be entertaining, they actually promote the value of being a tyrant and stigmatize empathy.

But why the stigma around empathy in the first place?

In my work traveling globally and interacting with different cultures, I've noticed that certain country groups have cultural norms in place. In many places, there are still gender stereotypes against showing emotion or having empathy.

Let's look at a few examples:

- In Latin groups, there is a machismo culture.

- In Japan, "tatemae" refers to the public face people present to others, and by contrast, "honne" refers to their true feelings and desires.

- In Russia, there is a concept called "suffering and stoicism," associated with strength and resilience. This leads to a cultural norm of displaying a stern demeanor.

- There is a persistent cultural norm in the Middle East for showing a more reserved or formal demeanor in public settings.

Those are just a few. It doesn't always involve the culture of a country or region. It can also be the culture within specific companies. The leader's attitude toward empathy makes a huge difference in how others see the value of kindness, relationships, and collaboration.

This begs the question: Can you still be an effective leader if you're not wired to be an empathetic person—perhaps even if you're known as a colossal jerk?

Case in point: Steve Jobs was famously a jerk to people, yet built a great company. How do we reconcile this? It's important to remember that Jobs wasn't just non-empathic. His management style was also associated with burnout, high levels of stress, and a huge turnover rate among his employees. He acknowledged later in life that his abrasive behavior was not always effective, and he expressed regret for some of his past actions.

At a certain point, to be an effective leader, you need to create a great culture where you put people first. It's not just a matter of ethical or moral considerations. It can also have a significant effect on the success and longevity of a business to have a more motivated workforce.

That can greatly impact the people in your company, but it extends to your community as well. Since the community extends into the culture, those seemingly mundane decisions about how you treat people can radically influence countless lives.

In our final chapter, we'll look at this in more detail as we bring our metaphor of concentric circles to its natural conclusion, focusing on transforming the culture.

15

TRANSFORMING THE CULTURE

We're nearly at the end of our journey together. In *The Business Artist*, we have explored the dissonance that makes business so difficult today (Part 1), the melody showing the way (Part 2), and the harmony that gives us a blueprint for making a difference in the world (Part 3).

To bring our journey to a close, I'll offer a few thoughts on how we can bring these themes together to impact the culture. Whatever you create on your own, with collaborators, in your company, and within your community has repercussions far beyond what you can do as an individual.

Inviting Conversations as a Business Artist

We live in an increasingly polarized culture. It's not only politics. In the realms of religion, education, entertainment, and more, it seems like the fringes are getting all the attention. On every conceivable topic, there is pressure to take a stand or call out a perceived enemy.

Much of this extremism is driven by social media. Remember, though, that 10 percent of users create 80 percent of the content. Think about that for a moment. If the majority of content is created by a small but influential minority of people with strong opinions, it will create a larger population that has strong opinions, and they will naturally divide into tribes. The social minority is perceived as a majority. Since most of us will go to great lengths to avoid conflict, we just go along with it.

We also need to understand how conformity bias plays into this. Essentially, it means we will adjust our opinion to go along with the crowd. Most parents have had some version of the following argument with their teens:

Parent: "You shouldn't do that!"

Teen: "But everybody's doing it, and therefore it must be okay!"

Parent: "If everybody was jumping off a bridge, would you do it, too? Just because everyone's doing something doesn't make it right. Sometimes the crowd is wrong."

It's not only teens who are prone to groupthink. We all do it. Tribalism is embedded so deeply into our DNA that it's almost impossible to escape it. We naturally fear people outside our tribes, whether that tribe is religious, political, geographic, or ethnic. Depending on the values within the tribe, tribe leaders can come down hard on dissenters and people who express divergent opinions.

It's why the idea of self-expression gets attacked by a vocal minority that wants you to believe a majority actually believes something you don't. In any social situation, a small minority of people are the loudest. They set the rules for the group, then let conformity bias do the rest.

This is why we need more respectful disagreement in culture. Business Artists can lead the way by inviting conversation rather than always having polarizing or divisive opinions. These conversations can happen within the tribe itself or with people from other tribes.

As an artist, I believe self-expression is a good thing! But there are ways to express yourself that draw others in and invite dialogue and ways to express yourself that push people away and invite division. I prefer the first!

If you want to impact the biggest group of people, you need to be able to relate to people who are different than you. That calls for diplomacy, empathy, understanding, patience, and, above all, a good dose of humility.

Why Do We Do This?

If you want to transform the culture and have an impact on the world, it doesn't start with a big vision (although that's important). It begins by looking inside yourself and asking a simple yet powerful question: "Why am I drawn to the type of work I do?"

You're probably drawn in a particular direction for dozens of reasons. I'll leave that to the psychologists to figure out. But at the end of the day, the single most important reason you're pulled toward a particular type of work is because it feeds your soul.

Maybe it's sales, design, writing, finance, HR, entrepreneurship, media, or one of a hundred other areas. If you enjoy your work, it's because it gives you joy on a fundamental level. I believe it's essential to connect with that source regularly. On any given day, there are projects to manage, people to talk to, and messages coming at you from a half-dozen different platforms. It's easy to lose the connection with the very thing that drew you to your creative work in the first place.

Harper Lee, the author of *To Kill a Mockingbird*, said, "Any writer worth his salt writes to please himself ... It's a self-exploratory operation that is endless. An exorcism of not necessarily his demon, but of his divine discontent."

The concept of *discontent* doesn't just apply to writers. Every artist creates because it fills a need in themselves. You might create for the market, for clients, or your company. But when it comes down to it, you're creating because you *can't not* create. It's part of your wiring as a Business Artist.

How do we express this desire, this internal need to create? These are some of the most common reasons artists do creative work. This is not an exhaustive list, but my guess is that you will see yourself in most of these.

We create to express ourselves. One of the fundamental differences between humans and the rest of the animal kingdom is that we have a psychological need to express hopes, dreams, individuality, and emotions. At our core, we want to be known. Art has always been a way to make those things known and, in the process, hopefully connect with others.

We create to experiment. There are endless ways to do this. We experiment with different visual elements; for example, you've got an ordinary presentation you want to enhance with images, words, movements, and colors. We experiment with the qualities of a particular medium; stage, meeting, presentation, video, and even email. We experiment by improvising and collaborating; to bring in new ideas, inspirations, and diverse perspectives.

We create to provoke. Do you feel uncomfortable with the word "provoke"? If so, that's the point. Provocation is meant to make people a little uncomfortable and to arouse a response. You can provoke for all kinds of reasons, such as starting a discussion, making people think, stirring up debate, or asking questions when you know there's no good answer. Sometimes, *shock and awe* is the best way to get someone's attention.

We create to teach. Business Artists enjoy using different verbal or written methods to help people grow and learn. Nobody does this better than Disney. When you visit one of their theme parks, multiple senses are engaged at the same time. In fact, Walt Disney required at least three senses to be engaged everywhere in the original park. Clearly, the designers have continued to follow this principle in all their parks. You may not be as big as Disney, but you can use the same principles. How can you combine sight and sound more effectively than just using traditional written and verbal messages?

We create to tell stories. We've talked about storytelling at length in this book, but I mention it again here because it's such a vital part of our creative work. Tell stories using your own tools, strengths, and techniques, all in service of the customer or client. I also encourage you to lean into visual storytelling. Long before humans had widespread literacy, we were painting on cave walls and telling stories through images on stained glass.

We create to empower. Creative action can advance a community or movement. Movements depend on symbols, images, stories, and other creative mediums to survive. Think about all the cultural upheaval of the 1960s. Can you imagine how much less potent it would have been without the music of that time?

I'm willing to believe that you see yourself in many of these themes. I hope they remind you why you're an artist in the first place and give you the strength to continue growing.

Why? Because growth is one of the main qualities of a Business Artist. If you're not growing, you're regressing. In a world where everything changes at such a fast pace, we have to do the hard work of growth, which means rewiring the very way we see ourselves and the world.

Rewiring Yourself

One of the most important traits of Business Artists is that we pursue *out-of-the-box* thinking, or what is sometimes called a "reality distortion field." Steve Jobs was famous for this. He would insist on having things a certain way or casting a vision that seemed impossible to create in the real world. However, that sense of *distorting reality* is precisely what helped him become such an influential figure in business.

Some artists are wired to think outside the box and take risks. But what if you're simply not wired that way?

While out-of-the-box thinking and having a reality distortion field is part of my *raison d'etre*, (reason for being) I know many people don't naturally see the world that way. That said, I believe it is a skill that can be cultivated over time if you're willing to give yourself permission.

But first, you need to get over your natural tendency to do things the way you've always done them. This is a big hurdle for most people and must be overcome for any real divergent thinking to occur. It's hard to suspend your self-judgment and silence the alarm that goes off inside your head whenever you try to change.

It's good to ask yourself, "Why am I thinking this way? Could there be alternatives? Am I dissatisfied enough with the current reality or where I'm heading to embrace a new mental pathway for a moment?" If you can mentally get to *yes,* then it's time to take action.

How? By learning, researching, and being open to new ideas. It means taking inspiration from different fields to see if you can make connections between seemingly unrelated concepts, disciplines, hobbies, or experiences. You must also challenge areas of this project or idea that have been done a certain way before, then get input from people with different skill sets and perspectives.

Then, when you're ready, start to narrow down your new ideas. I like to daydream about new ideas and *play them out a bit* to see what could happen if you take experiments to their natural conclusions. I'd also suggest getting into a habit of experimenting with some of the ideas that seem feasible. Make sure to put your own stamp of artistry on this.

And finally, save your work! Track what you tried this time and what didn't go well. When you need to think outside the box again, you'll have previous ideas to review (and sometimes laugh at later)!

Those are a handful of ideas that any Business Artist can put into practice. But what about companies? I'd like to take the remainder of this closing chapter and reflect on some ways leaders can make a big difference for their team members and, ultimately, the whole culture.

Working with a Purpose

The world of work has changed dramatically over the last couple of decades due to massive advances in technology and the opportunities for remote work. We're in the middle of a giant revolution questioning all aspects of work and rethinking our assumptions about how it should take place.

One thing that won't change, however, is the need for purpose. No matter what type of work someone's doing, they want to know that their work has purpose. They want to feel they are contributing to something important and that their efforts have meaning beyond just getting a paycheck. This is essential if a worker is to stay committed to their employer.

Unfortunately, many companies are far behind this ideal because they are stuck in old ways of thinking developed by Fredrik Taylor, the father of modern scientific management, whom I've mentioned earlier in the book. He was a huge advocate for productivity and taught that employees should essentially be treated like machines.

It sounds good on paper, and it's a great strategy for getting many things built in a factory with more efficiency and profitability. However, this philosophy of employment resulted in de-skilled employees who were seen as expendable. If you only do one small thing of the whole task, you can be replaced much easier.

Some companies started to go further than his advice and didn't pay employees more (except Henry Ford, who paid double for highly effective workers, which led to great success for years and years). It created a harsh work environment where everything revolved around the survival of the fittest. Employees suffered burnout, dehumanization, and mental anguish as they were separated from the greater purpose of their work.

For well over one hundred years, this approach to work has been the standard in the developed world. Why? Because historically, we have valued profitability over almost everything else. However, the practices that made profitability and growth possible in a factory setting are now outdated and need to be balanced with a responsibility to people.

I would argue that employees have more opportunities to have purpose now than in the past, but it is still not enough. There are systems and processes companies can implement, but it is more the responsibility of the employee to find purpose than it is for the employer to give it to them. That said, companies today need to foster a culture where this is possible.

I often find disengaged colleagues or friends who have a fixed mindset (instead of a growth mindset) when it comes to purpose. A growth mindset is essential for finding purpose in work because it allows employees to see challenges and setbacks as opportunities for learning and to take ownership of their career development. Instead, they believe the company is against them, or that they'll never get promoted. Therefore, they are less likely to take risks, learn from mistakes, and embrace challenges.

I love Maya Angelou's quote: "If you don't like something, change it. If you can't change it, change your attitude." I know that sounds simple, but those are words that artists live by every day.

Every Job is a Learning Opportunity

Another way that businesses can bring transformation into the workplace is to build learning into every job. I mentioned this briefly early in the chapter, but let's explore this a bit more.

The trend these days is toward self-paced training when someone begins a new job. You've probably used resources from companies like Lynda, Degreed, or LinkedIn Learning. They are cheap and efficient and, therefore, have become the default way to train people for a while now.

In my thirteen years in the learning consulting space, I can attest to how inefficient self-paced learning is when it is pushed on people, with the exception of a few areas, such as learning and practicing sales skills, which can be done well via AI. The best innovation and strategy learning happens through peer-to-peer collaboration in person or virtual workshops.

I love workshops because they allow employees to learn from each other. Those settings also foster greater teamwork and collaboration. Part of the reason I left my consulting career is that I didn't see many great ways for individual employees, managers, or leaders to effectively create and deliver meaningful workshops outside of using PowerPoint, simple polling, or whiteboarding software.

There is untapped creativity within every employee. They can share their creativity with each other and bring in people from the outside who can share their knowledge. Education shouldn't be reserved for learning and development teams to provide exclusively.

We have to expand how we think of education. Learning doesn't have to happen in a formal education setting. On-the-job feedback in a constructive manner is critical to ensure everyone has a voice when it comes to collaboration.

Continuing education is important and can be individualized. I'm a big fan of YouTube and reading new authors to feed my mind with new ideas. I hope that in reading this book, you have learned things that you can take forward for yourself and share with others.

I encourage you to be original! Nothing is more aggravating to me than seeing someone become an avatar of another leader. As a Business Artist, it's important to take inspiration from learning, but be cautious about how much you parrot what you hear from others. Challenge what you read and learn. There is no *how-to guide* that any author, leader, or YouTuber wants you to follow verbatim. You can learn from everyone and everything, then take it all in to shape your own perspective.

Learning is not absolute. It is subjective, contextual, ongoing, and always subject to revision and improvement. What we know today may be proven false or incomplete tomorrow as new information and insights are gained. Therefore, we must be open to questioning and challenging our assumptions and beliefs and be willing to update our knowledge and understanding.

This is one of the reasons I co-founded Meahana.io, a software company with a focus on enabling facilitators (which can be any employee) to be better at creating and delivering content—whether it is theirs, ours, or from our third-party marketplace of content providers.

Our no-code platform was built by facilitators for facilitators who want to unleash their creativity in ways they can't with today's tools or without large consulting budgets. It also features templates and activities that are easy to access and customize.

Building this company has been a shift for me since I spent so many years as a designer of experiences, builder of content, and facilitator of workshops and training. Now, I am enabling creators to do all of this in a more self-serving way where we can learn from them over time.

Breaking the Rules

As you have seen throughout this book, I'm a big fan of challenging the status quo and breaking the rules when necessary. But how does a leader handle an employee who is constantly breaking the rules and being disruptive or not helpful? How do you know when it's breaking the rules for innovation versus breaking the rules because someone isn't a team player or is uncooperative?

In this case, I believe there needs to be an assessment of motivation and the root cause when someone breaks the rules. Most of the time, it is because they are trying to be innovative and creative. However, there may be instances where they have a personal agenda causing them to break the current rules.

In the workplace, I often find that the rules weren't *set* to begin with, and there is only pushback when someone has done something differently. To combat this, managers must constantly remind themselves to set performance and behavior expectations. Make sure the employee understands these and what is expected of them, and the consequences of not meeting those expectations. Expectations are the necessary constraints toward good creativity from your team. When you put limiting constraints on someone, it doesn't necessarily limit creativity. In fact, it often does quite the opposite.

Don't be shy about asking for specific expectations upfront. Don't be afraid to challenge the expectations if you feel a different approach or outcome would work better. The key is to get a clear agreement.

The last thing you want is for your manager to expect a ten-page proposal with an executive summary, you spend all week making a fun video instead and then get a stern response. It would have been much better to have said, "I want to try something new—maybe a video format first. If it doesn't work, let's go back to a written proposal format."

Good communication in a business setting is key, just like in any other setting where we relate with people. Once expectations are set, giving feedback on what someone is doing well is easier than expressing what needs improvement.

A Few Closing Thoughts

Pablo Picasso said, "The purpose of art is washing the dust of daily life off our souls." Art in all its forms, including when it's used in business, has the power to break down boundaries and bridge distances between people. Creativity can wash the dust of worn-out assumptions and outdated practices from how we do business.

Humans are the only species on planet Earth that creates art. We have an amazing capacity for creative thinking. We see it in science, technology, business, education, and every other domain of culture. Why should the world of business be any different?

Maybe it's time to change our thinking. Instead of thinking that business is the last setting where we should use art and creative thinking, maybe it should be the first.

My wife, Chrissi, who is a creative art director, received some great advice that helped propel her career. "Treat every project as if it was going to go in your portfolio." She told me this changed her mindset and allowed her to approach each project as a reflection of herself.

This is true for all of us. Everything we do in life and business matters. All your actions impact someone else in some way, big or small. It might be the customer you're serving directly, the colleague you're supporting, or the end user of the product you're creating for a client. It could be a shareholder you'll never meet personally or a random person in another country who benefits from the boost in their economy because your company did business with a company in their country.

The world of business doesn't just benefit from your creativity. The world *needs* your creativity. Everything you do is part of your life's portfolio that you ultimately show to the world.

As a Business Artist, I can't think of a better way for you to spend your time and creative energy.

ENDNOTES

Chapter 4

1.   Prof. Dr. Francisco Tigre Moura, "David Cope: A Lifetime Contribution to Artificial Intelligence and Music," *LiveInnovation.org*, November 19, 2018. https://liveinnovation.org/david-cope-a-lifetime-contribution-to-artificial-intelligence-and-music.

Chapter 5

2.   Jackie Wiles, "New documentary shows creativity is the key to greatness," *Gartner*, January 26, 2023, https://www.gartner.com/en/articles/beyond-chatgpt-the-future-of-generative-ai-for-enterprises.

Chapter 6

3.   Yuval Noah Harari, *Homo Deus: A Brief History of Tomorrow* (New York: HarperCollins, 2017).

4.   Jim Grove, "New documentary shows creativity is the key to greatness," *Active for Life,* November 14, 2018, https://activeforlife. com/new-documentary-shows-creativity-is-key-to-greatness.

Chapter 7

5.   Noomi Matlow, "More Kairos, Less Chronos (Live More. Work Less)," *Unsettled,* https://beunsettled.co/blog/more-kairos-less-chronos-live-more-work-less.

6.   Steven Pressfield, *The War of Art: Break Through the Blocks and Win Your Inner Creative Battles* (New York: Black Irish Entertainment LLC, 2002).

Chapter 8

7.   Mihaly Csikszentmihalyi, *Flow: The Psychology of Optimal Experience* (New York: Harper Perennial Modern Classics, 2008).

8.   Scott Barry Kaufman, "The Real Neuroscience of Creativity," *Scientific American*, August 19, 2013, https://blogs.scientificamerican.com/beautiful-minds/the-real-neuroscience-of-creativity/.

Chapter 9

9.   Ella Miron-Spektor, Miriam Erez, and Eitan Naveh, "To Drive Creativity, Add Some Conformity," *Harvard Business Review*, March 2012, https://hbr.org/2012/03/to-drive-creativity-add-some-conformity.

10. Jeff Bezos, "Jeff Bezos At The Economic Club Of Washington," September 13, 2018, YouTube video, 41:1, https://www.youtube.com/watch?v=xv_vkA0jsyo.

11. Maric, A., Montvai, E., Werth, E., Storz, M., Leemann, J., Weissengruber, S., Ruff, C. C., Huber, R., Poryazova, R., & Baumann, C. R., "Insufficient sleep: Enhanced risk-seeking relates to low local sleep intensity," *Annals of Neurology*, 82(3), 409-418, https://doi.org/10.1002/ana.25023.

Chapter 10

12. Brandt Ranj and Alyson Shontell, "10 insanely successful co-founders and why their partnerships worked," *Business Insider*, January 21, 2016. https://www.businessinsider.com/10-successful-cofounders-and-why-their-partnerships-worked.

Chapter 11

13. Stephen R. Covey, *The 7 Habits of Highly Effective People: 30th Anniversary Edition* (New York: Simon & Schuster, 2020).

14. You can access your own CliftonStrengths for Sales at https://www.gallup.com/cliftonstrengths/en/392279/cliftonstrengths-for-sales.aspx.

15. Jeff Bezos, *Invent and Wander: The Collected Writings of Jeff Bezos* (Boston: Harvard Business Review Press, 2020).

16. Gloria Mark, "Doing Nothing Can Make You More Productive," *Time*, February 11, 2023, https://time.com/6254135/doing-nothing-more-productive.

17. Matt Walker, "Sleep is your superpower | Matt Walker," June 3, 2019, https://www.youtube.com/watch?v=5MuIMqhT8DM.

Chapter 12

18. Todd Rose, *Collective Illusions: Conformity, Complicity, and the Science of Why We Make Bad Decisions* (New York: Hachette Go, 2022). You can access the Big Think YouTube channel at https://www.youtube.com/@bigthink.

19. Todd Rose, "Psychologist debunks 8 myths of mass scale | Todd Rose," December 4, 2022, https://www.youtube.com/watch?v=BD_Euf_CBbs.

Chapter 13

20. Mathias Benedekl and Aljoscha C Neubauer1, "Revisiting Mednick's Model on Creativity-Related Differences in Associative Hierarchies. Evidence for a Common Path to Uncommon Thought," *The Journal of Creative Behavior*, November 15, 2013, https://www.ncbi.nlm.nih.gov/pmc/articles/PMC3924568.

WOULD YOU KINDLY REVIEW THIS BOOK?

If you enjoyed this book, would you consider taking a moment to leave a review where you purchased it? I would be grateful. Thank you!

ACKNOWLEDGMENTS

To my former employer, BTS, unique in its model of the *triple threat*, where consultants get to sell, develop, and deliver their own projects. It's an insane model that attracts and retains some of the brightest people I've ever met while fostering an unmatched creative culture that instills trust and ownership between employees and their clients.

To the global sales enablement and management teams at SAP, Google, Autodesk, Splunk, Salesforce, Cisco, and others, for letting me innovate together with you, finding new creative solutions, and never settling for "what's been done before."

To Ryan Hickey, the first teacher of music who could help my mind break through and see the theory behind the art that unlocked a love for music appreciation.

To Peter Benassi, my first sales teacher. Peter's unorthodox approach was never to ensure the repeatability of the process, but to ensure the repeatability of success. In a room of customers, he taught me to read the smallest expressions and improvise often.

To my mom and dad, thank you for raising me in a way that gave me the freedom to pursue my passions with a strong sense of what it means to live a dignified life.

To Kent Sanders, without whom this book would have sat as an idea for many more years. Thank you for guiding me as the "producer of my mind" and for the role you played in making this book happen.

To the other publishing experts who helped bring this book to life: Kristi Griffith (book cover and formatting designer), Karen Hunsanger (editor), and Jen Piceno (proofreader). Thank you for using your skills to bring *The Business Artist* to life.

To my three co-founders at Meahana—Matt, John, and Beth—for supporting my vision of the Business Artist as an overlapping mission to ours as we seek to empower and enable others through innovation.

To my wife, Chrissi, for giving me access to see the world through an artistic lens and for putting up with me talking about this book for the last three-plus years.

ABOUT THE AUTHOR

I'm Adam, a self-proclaimed social theorist who loves diving into the intricate workings of our world. I have a deep-seated passion for blending the beauty of artistic principles with technology, business, and society, unlocking fascinating new viewpoints along the way.

The book you're reading, *The Business Artist*, has been my labor of love over the past few years. Drawing from my time as a consultant, I've seen firsthand how artistic principles differentiate top performers in business. But there's a challenge: balancing the appeal of creativity and innovation against the comfort of data-driven certainty.

In a similar vein, I recently launched Meahana.io, a platform that shares this mission. Both are designed to ignite your creativity, giving you the tools you need to steer your artistic vision.

I had a great American upbringing. I was born in Phoenix, Arizona, then moved to Indiana when I was nine. My family—a teacher mom, a salesman dad, and my three siblings—shaped me and my outlook on life.

Art captured my heart in my middle and high school music theater days. Over time, that love grew to encompass all forms of art.

After completing my computer and management degrees at Purdue, I relocated to Los Angeles, where I met Chrissi Hernandez, my beautiful wife. A talented art major and designer, Chrissi broadened my understanding of the artistic world, revealing how the use of light, composition, and aesthetics can provoke emotion.

Living with Chrissi has taught me an important lesson. *Everyone is capable of artistic expression.* Seriously, living with an artist will change the way you see things.

This revelation, combined with my professional background, inspired me to start my mental output into voice memos, hundreds of observational research notes, and eventually writing *The Business Artist.* The book champions the idea that everyone, like renowned directors or AI tools interpreting the same script, has their unique style and artistic potential, especially in professional roles.

Technology has always been a strong interest of mine. My friends would call me a tinkerer. From disassembling desktops in the mid-90s to co-founding a computer networking business in high school, I've always been right there as technology evolved. My tinkering continues in music and DJing to this day under the name DJ Street Meat.

My extensive technology experience and time spent co-creating workshops with pioneering tech companies culminated in Meahana's inception. We saw a clear need for a platform that would enable leaders to create their own workshops, unhampered by the wrong tools. So, we made Meahana a platform where simplicity meets sophistication, unlocking the inner facilitator in everyone. It really is like an artist's studio for professionals to collaborate in new and exciting ways.

Want to keep this conversation going? Visit Meahana.io to sign up for our bi-weekly Business Artist Insiders email featuring regular updates and exclusive content. The Business Artist Movement is focused on nurturing the artist within every professional.

Together, we can explore this unique mindset and make a real difference.

Made in the USA
Columbia, SC
16 September 2024

41954619R00133